ANGELS

IN SADR CITY

We Remember...

COMMEMORATIVE EDITION (2021)

ANGELS

IN SADR CITY

WE REMEMBER

COMMEMORATIVE EDITION (2021)

Traitmarker Books
2984 Del Rio Pike
Franklin, TN 37069
traitmarkerbooks.com
traitmarker@gmail.com

Interior Text Font: Minion Pro
Interior Title Fonts: Minion Pro
Editor: Robbie Grayson III

Printed in the United States of America

TABLE OF CONTENTS

Foreword: by Hollie McKay   *vii*

Preface: by John Reyes   *xv*

CHAPTER 1—*The War on Terror Emerges*   *1*

CHAPTER 2— *COP Ford*   *13*

CHAPTER 3—*The Price Paid*   *23*

CHAPTER 4—*The Battle for Route Gold*   *35*

CHAPTER 5—*A Recon Team Leader's Story*   *65*

CHAPTER 6—*Battle for Sadr City*   *95*

CHAPTER 7—*Horse*   *107*

Tributes   *116*

CHAPTER 8—*Bravo Intersection*   *126*

CHAPTER 9—*Reunion*   *145*

CHAPTER 10—*Delta Intersection*   *156*

CHAPTER 11—*Tactical Operations Center*   *168*

CHAPTER 12— *Support of the Families*   *188*

CHAPTER 13—*The Personal Trial*   *194*

CHAPTER 14—*A Soldier's Thoughts*   *201*

CHAPTER 15—*After Action Report*   *216*

Memoirs   *231*

SWET: Boone Cutler   *233*

No One Ever Hurt Us Without Payback: Greg Baker   *241*

The Worst Day: Logan Veath   *245*

A February Raid in the War on Terror: Jarrod Taylor   *277*

The Sadr City Connection: Scott Wolfe   *297*

Sadr City: The Music Video

HOLLIE
MCKAY

FOREWORD
BY HOLLIE McKAY

Entering Sadr City is akin to entering a mutated gray universe, teetering somewhere on the edge of the earth.

The first thing that punches you is the smell—wild goats feasting on the trash decaying beneath the full tilt of the Baghdad heat, a cocktail of blood and urine seeping out onto the broad and broken roads. The next is the sounds, a chorus of constant car honks and the shrilling, infant-like screams of poultry burned alive in the open slaughterhouses.

Officially termed the "Al-Thawra" district, Sadr City embodies the slums, home to the capital's most impoverished. More than three million inhabitants are stuffed into the neglected public housing projects. Electricity works just a few hours a day; water drips an evil yellow drip from the cracked taps.

But at the same time, it symbolizes the nation's resilience, of the working class whose lives have been defined by endless oppression, occupation, bloodletting and defiance.

In the ancient market that languishes next to the oversized poster of nationalist Shite cleric Moqtada al Sadr, inhabitants shuffle like ghosts in the daylight, some with visible wounds and some without. Some have stumps where their arms should be, and others kneel on the cold concrete deluged in animal feces to prepare their poultry for slaughter. There are grocers and spice sellers, artists and seamstresses.

Everybody works. Nobody complains.

During my first visit, a late 2017 fall afternoon—amid a strange blend of humidity and an early whip of winter wind slicing the smog—Sadr City hummed along as a Mahdi Army leader by the name of Moslem Salik escorted me, my black abaya dragging in the dust, through the dense crowds.

It reminded me of a place not quite at peace, yet no longer at war: a pock-marked mosaic of pride and struggle. One by one, the locals emerge from the shadows of their daily chores to tell stories.

"I have a normal life now. There are no problems," a beaming, fresh-faced twenty-five-year-old named Sadoon Aziz quipped from behind his bench, where he made cheese and yogurt like a sculptor perfecting his Madonna. "It is much better now than under the Americans. They were closing the streets, cutting the roads off, arresting people; now we are all living in the quiet."

Of course, Sadr City is eponymous with the protracted U.S.-occupation of Iraq in the dizzying aftermath of the September 11 attacks. It morphed into a hotbed of fighting and destruction, with the Mahdi militiamen rising up to slaughter and push out the American footprint from its unpaved terrain.

Sadr City is also an exemplar of the fraught challenges of nation-building. While the U.S. mandate was to repair the decayed civilian infrastructure, the ensuing years were made up of urban fights, city lockdowns, almost daily mortar rounds, RPGs crackling in the reeking air, the unearthing of shallow graves, and the sound of car bombs popping in every direction.

The Mahdi Army's will to defy foreign presence only gained momentum throughout the American troop surges of 2007 and 2008, when rockets relentlessly fired from Sadr City into the American-controlled Green Zone nearby.

I meandered through the markets and met Abbas, a forty-three-year-old selling seeds and nuts in the local market. His face and one side of his body were mangled by discoloration and deep scars, like tiny trenches dug into his rough skin. He proudly proclaimed that he was one of the many arrested by U.S. forces and held from 2003 to 2006 in the notorious Camp Bucca prison—the same prison that had once sheltered ISIS leader Abu al-Baghdadi, the most wanted man in the world.

"I was attacking the Americans here, so they arrested me," Abbas explained without remorse. "They found out my name and took me from my house to the jail and tortured me. You can see the signs of torture on my face and body."

I pressed him further on the torture allegations. The truth unraveled: he was not tortured but had gotten into a fight with the correctional officer. An uprising had stirred, and he was shot in the chaos.

Sadr City, built-in 1959 by then-Iraqi Prime Minister Abdul Karim Qassim to deal with drastic housing shortages in Baghdad and initially called "Revolution City," for decades thrived on that rebellious spirit and bitter history. It quickly contorted into an underground hub for Communist Party members and later attracted the vicious ire of dictator Saddam Hussein who endeavored to lay waste to the enclave's Shia resistance.

Yet there was little time for locals to celebrate his capture in the dawning days of 2003 as the U.S. Army had already established a base in an abandoned cigarette factory. From the resident's purview, that served merely as another pearl in their string of revolutions and wars.

I met an elderly lady named Saami in another market stall, who ran her fabric shop single-handedly for thirty years.

"During the Americans, I could not open my shop. Every day there were weapons," she said in a small, tough voice as wisps of her show-white hair fell from behind her black abaya and into her tired eyes. "But we are secure now; we live in peace now. We have the Iraqi Army, the Mahdi Army, the Popular Mobilization—all of them together give us peace."

While recollections of U.S. occupation were typically

not ones doused with happiness, some intellectuals of Sadr City had nothing but hope and praise for that era of their lives. Despite its rampant scarcity, Sadr City boasts some of Baghdad's most eloquent poets and free-thinkers, people who dig for suits and shiny shoes in the open pits of trash to look their best.

"I am a secular person. Trump now and all the American presidents before him, they are good men who want us to have a free and open society," Ismik al-Baghdadi, a local political writer and journalist, said softly over a sip of tea. "But the U.S. dream for an open society did not work in a country like Afghanistan, but it did in Japan. Maybe it is not too late for it to work here."

Nonetheless, Ismik looked through me earnestly, insisting that it was far from a place of loss. He smiled and tipped his feathered fedora as a token of appreciation for the conversation, then disappeared into the fouled streets. I watched him wander past the silhouettes of shattered things until he became a pleasant speck in my memory.

In 2010, as the U.S. readied to withdraw from the war-splattered country altogether, a Turkish consortium won an $11.3 billion bid to construct Sadr City, which included bringing to life a modern city of 75,000 housing units to accommodate up to 600,000 people.

"We don't want it," Moselm told me, his eyes flashing with gentle defiance as he stared out into the destitution that even rays of sunlight did not touch. "People here want to be left alone."

They did not want their family homes knocked down and replaced by something towering and shiny and unfamiliar.

According to my good Iraqi friend Rusly, who had just published a book about his country's rises and falls entitled *The Collapse,* Sadr City is—and always would be—run by tribal law, not legislation dished out by the Central Government.

"Other tribes will punish for hurting someone; people know this, and that is why the crimes have stopped in Sadr City," he surmised.

Only the revolts have not. In 2019, as the streets of Iraq's south lit up with protests, a desperate bid to stamp out government corruption and a growing Iranian influence, Sadr City also became a kind of ground-zero for the pent-up frustrations of the poor who saw no support from a government that purported to protect them.

Chaos again reigned as Tehran-connected militias opened fire on the faces and frames of Sadr City. Yet the locals—filled with fortitude—hit back.

Perhaps it is that willingness to face danger, to fight for their perceived sense of freedom, never to surrender, that has wormed into the hearts and minds of the many thousands of U.S. personnel who came of age in Sadr City. I understood why some of my U.S. soldier friends still had something of an odd affection for the fractured place. I felt that there was something there that they all should know.

Oddly, their mission in Sadr City had been completed.

Since the U.S. occupation, their leader Moqtada al Sadr had slowly redefined himself from a religious hardliner to a controversial, albeit populist patriot, a constant preacher of accord and harmony. He even changing his militia's name to the Peace Brigades—and mandated his many die-hard followers lay down their arms.

"Sadr orders everyone not to talk about their own party and their own tribe. But all of us, we listen to him. We go to Friday prayers; we teach lessons of peace in the school," vowed Moslem. "We are not scared from terrorists. Some of the simple people still worry about their businesses, but we will protect them with peace."

Indeed, Sadr City today remains ready to defend its perfectly imperfect place.

HOLLIE MCKAY | JUNE 2021
ONLY CRY FOR THE LIVING, AUTHOR

SFC JOHN
I. REYES

PREFACE
BY JOHN REYES

I would like to dedicate this book to my mother, Raquel Reyes, who recently passed away from pancreatic cancer. Rest in peace, Mother (November 22, 1955-March 14, 2012). You will be greatly missed and loved. You were strong, having four kids in the military and at one point having all of us kids deployed. Your strength helped me a lot through deployments.

To my friends and family, thanks for being there during the passing of my mother. My mother had what is called tough love. Her being that way made me the man I am now: never have I smoked, taken a sip of alcohol or liquor, or done drugs. She taught me right from wrong throughout my life.

I would like to thank my dad, Juan Ramon Reyes. He is a strong supporter of the military. His dad and my grandfather, Ramon Reyes, started it all for our family by serving in the Korean War.

I would like to thank my brothers, Ramon Reyes III, Roger Reyes, and my sister, Cristina Reyes.

I've been in the military for 10 years, serving in Korea (2002-2003), Fort Lewis (2003-2006), Germany (2006-

2009), Fort Polk (2009-2010), and currently stationed at Fort Carson, Colorado. You can have your say about the military, but I have no regrets.

I've met people from all around the world. And even though my Army job is infantry (which is to kill bad guys), I have enjoyed helping those in need during the wars in Iraq and Afghanistan. I knew what I was getting into when I raised my right hand to be in the military. No one said it was going to be a walk in the park. I knew I was going to war, and I mentally prepared myself to be able to fight the enemy and to show no weakness to my soldiers.

I enjoy life a lot, and never will I take anything for granted. I try to do good deeds daily by opening a door for someone, by saying thanks, or by doing favors. I would like everyone to try to do something good daily, every day, for the remainder of your lives. Maybe people will appreciate life more.

Life is what you make of it. It's hard when you make it hard and easy and enjoyable when you make it that way. It's your life. Everything you choose in your life is your decision. Deployment helped me greatly by not letting me take everything thrown at me in life for granted. And for that, I would like to say thank you to all my brothers in arms with whom I have served and have fought shoulder-to-shoulder during my deployments.

JOHN REYES | MARCH 2021

SGT BERRY, OLIVER
DIED 5 JULY 2016

SPC O'HARA, FRANCIS
DIED 2 NOV 2012

SGT HEEKIN, CHARLES
DIED 26 MARCH 2015

Currently, I'm now a Sergeant First Class (SFC) at Fort Carson, Colorado and set to retire Jan 2022. My main focus post retirement is to help and guide veterans in how to beat PTSD, in how to find an escape, and in how to gain back that brotherhood and sense of purpose. Too many soldiers leave service and feel lost. They feel like they don't have a purpose. My advice to them is to get involved within their communities. Volunteer. Join non-profit veteran organizations like Team Rubicon, Team Red White and Blue (RWB), The Mission Continues, Wounded Warrior Project, etc. Regain that feeling of purpose and service. Do it by joining other like-minded people, by giving back, and by having the camaraderie again.

SFC JOHN I. REYES

T<small>RAITMARKER</small> B<small>OOKS</small> | *Franklin, TN*

To
#sadrcityboys
EVERYWHERE

This story shall the good man
teach his son... from this day
to the ending of the world,
But we in it shall be remember'd
We few, we happy few,
we band of brothers;
For he today that sheds his blood
with me shall be my brother...

HENRY V
Shakespeare

SGT ANTHONY
FARINA

1

THE WAR ON TERROR EMERGES

MY career in the United States military began with a four-year tour in the Marine Corps where I trained and deployed with the infantry and later with a reconnaissance unit. The Marines gave me the opportunity to visit 18 countries that included four major deserts.

During my last deployment in the Marines, I was with a small detachment doing recon patrols from August through September 2001 from an outpost about 15 miles from the infamous Camp Bondsteel, in Kosovo. We were conducting a lot of these patrols due to criminal activity in our area, and short routes from villages to our outpost were needed in case of an emergency and to seclude the transfer of prisoners.

I remember this tour well and the events that took place one particular day. Upon completing a 19-hour recon patrol, I came back to the squad tent to rest. An hour later, Lieutenant Regan busted into the tent and awoke everyone by yelling that the World Trade Centers had been hit.

"Get up! Get up! Out of your cots now! The World Trade Centers have been hit by terrorists! They are gone!"

Groggily, I said "But Sir, we came off a 19-hour patrol an hour or so ago, can't we fight more bad guys later?"

"Look, this isn't a time to joke around, Corporal Farina," Regan retorted. "This is a serious situation. Now get all the men up while I gather details on what we are doing next."

I was so young and naive at that time that I had no clue what the World Trade Centers were, so I rolled over and fell back asleep. Later when I awoke, I was informed of the situation, and everything sank in. Little did I know that one single act of terrorism would bring me to Iraq in 2003 and back again in the winter of 2007 along with the dawn of a new age in warfare. Though there were many great trials in the Marines, I left the Corps in June of 2002 with my heart unsatisfied.

Two weeks after my discharge from the Marines, I found myself in the Army, seeking out the elite United States Army Special Forces, known as the Green Berets. Amidst the long escalation of claims and preparation I deployed to Kuwait as part of the invasion force, and my plans for the Green Berets were delayed.

During my time in Iraq in 2003, I had the pleasure of serving with some of the noblest men in the Army. Four of these men lost their lives to a suicide bomber, the first such act of a war that went on for a little over ten years.

One of the fondest memories of this tour was when I stood my ground during my first hostile engagement. There were about eight men on the ground along with two Abrams battle tanks and one Bradley fighting vehicle. Our short mission was to block all traffic leaving Baghdad and to allow anyone wishing to enter the city to proceed. We were on the main highway that runs through Iraq known as Highway 8.

As day turned to night and our perimeter became established, the men on the ground started detaining people from vehicles, putting them in holding areas surrounded in concertina wire. Swerving down the road, a truck came speeding towards the checkpoint.

Some of the men tried to flag the truck down and get them to stop. For some reason the truck did not stop. As soon as it crossed a designated line, everyone on the ground opened fire.

Within moments the vehicle came to a halt. Upon inspection the bodies of two teenage boys, mutilated from a spray of bullets, and a wounded woman were revealed. The woman was helped from the vehicle and given medical attention.

While she was being treated, the ground crew assessed damage, only to react to fire from a distant tree-line two hundred meters away.

Bursting into the air, two RPGs shot through the night sky and somehow weaved their way through the two main battle tanks stationed in the middle of the road. I remember the first one clearly, because it shot over my head. The heat signature it left behind is still fresh in my mind.

As all of the men on the ground were taking cover and trying to identify the position from where the enemy was attacking us, another rocket took flight and landed in the dirt. This particular rocket landed next to the head of a fellow soldier. I remember that our eyes locked in disbelief because the rocket landed, glowed red for a minute, and then lost its color.

More rockets started to come in along with a hail of bullets from all directions. The men stood their ground, returned fire and began to maneuver to cover and gain good fighting positions. As everyone was returning fire across the main road, I noticed my friend, Kyle Hartley, was tangled up in the concertina wire. As karma would have it, this was the same wire used to detain the individuals from the vehicles stopped earlier that night.

Running to his side, I began pulling at the wire with my bare hands. He was tangled like a marionette, trying to move in one direction while the rest of his body remained trapped. After a few minutes, two of my leaders assisted me in getting him out of his predicament. At this moment the two individuals trying to free Kyle and me

4

became the center of attention for our enemies.

Rounds impacted by our feet, throwing bits of sand in the air and into my eyes. No sooner did Kyle get free than a large number of RPGs exploded onto the scene, heading in our direction. Those of us who were being fired upon maneuvered, finding good positions to return fire. Once we were set, the tanks and Bradley started engaging the tree line where the enemy was attacking.

The fight was soon over.

When all was calm, I looked over to Kyle and saw he was okay. I asked him for some water, because I had dropped mine while cutting him loose and my other one was empty. He told me he didn't have but a swallow left of his own supply. However, because I came to him in his time of need, he gave me his last drop.

This was the first time ever that I had seen the true bond of men in combat. A brother giving his last drop of water after risking your life for him: that is what makes being out there worth it. It's the hell and close-calls you endure together that make the bond so unbreakable in combat.

Days went by before the first suicide bombing of the entire war. It was Saturday, March 29, 2003. Around 10 a.m. the infantry platoon to which I was assigned and with which I had trained for a year received orders to provide relief for the other men in our company at the checkpoint our platoon secured the previous night.

Four Bradleys rolled up to the checkpoint. The ramps from the vehicles dropped, and the men from the platoon took up different positions in a 360-degree perimeter. Four men, SGT Eugene Williams, PVT Michael Creighton, CPL Michael Curtin, and PFC Diego Rincon were instructed to relieve a four-man team that stood in the middle of Hwy. 8, inspecting a vehicle that had been stopped.

While they proceeded to the checkpoint, SPC Hartley (with whom I fought in the battle the night before) and I took up a machine gun position to the right of SGT Williams' team's location. Hartley and I were about 75 meters away from the middle of the highway. We set up a machine gun nest and started to draw a sketch of our sector to gain a clear idea of where our firing line both began and ended.

As Hartley was drawing, I looked over to see CPL Curtin bring the driver of a small cab with a white front and orange back to the rear of the vehicle. I watched how the man exited the vehicle and complied with CPL Curtin's orders. SGT Williams was on the passenger side of the vehicle while PVT Creighton and PFC Rincon were towards the front, pulling security.

As I watched CPL Curtin lead the man to the trunk of the vehicle, I got a quick look at Diego. Fond memories flashed through my head from times back at Ft. Stewart, Georgia (the base we deployed from) when I used to teach Diego how to cook. I smiled as I remembered the first time I helped him, because he wanted nothing more than to cook for his girlfriend.

6

A loud explosion shattered that memory. The eruption was so heavy and strong that it stopped me from breathing, and I fell over. I went deaf, silence consuming my sense of hearing.

Time slowed as the air filled with black smoke and debris from the blast smacked my face. I buried my head in the ground, because I immediately thought our position had been compromised by the enemy and I expected incoming artillery at any moment.

Hartley would later tell me that for about 30 seconds, I had a look of ultimate fear on my face and did not move. I cannot recall this, but I don't doubt it. I went from remembering a fond memory one moment to watching four of my brothers disappear in the middle of a billowing cloud of fire and smoke.

Snapping out of confusion, I saw men running to provide aid to the wounded. SPC Dustin Wheeland, a close friend and fellow soldier, rushed to Rincon, putting him in his lap while stanching the blood gushing from his neck. Rincon was gasping for air, but he could not take any in.

Creighton had received equally devastating injuries to his backside. SGT Williams was dealt the same fate. Michael Curtin was another story. The men searched for him during the chaos, but they could only find his torso, secured in his body armor. That was it, nothing more was left. His dog tags would later be found 100 meters from the blast site.

All of this took place in a few minutes. Then gunfire broke out in all directions. The tanks and Bradleys were firing on multiple targets that attempted to attack our position. The fighting lasted about ten minutes, then all was quiet. This incident would forever be known as the first suicide bombing of the entire war in Iraq. It was announced to all on the ground at the checkpoint a few hours later.

I often held guilt inside because Curtin had my job. Back in Ft. Stewart prior to leaving for Iraq, I was in his position as a team leader. I was asked if I wanted to deploy with the unit or seek out Special Forces. When I answered that I wanted to seek out Special Forces, I was told that the question was a test of my loyalty and that I would be downgraded to a machine gunner. CPL Curtin took my place as a team leader. He took my spot, and I will always remember and be grateful for this man.

Diego Rincon's death was critical in creating a new law that would help future immigrants gain citizenship by joining the U.S. military. This, as I will speak of later, is the reason why revenge was a key emotion in battle: having a good memory of an old friend ripped out of your mind, only to see him die. It's a price paid through war for freedom of a country that all soldiers love.

The loss of my brothers drove me to continue with my plan to join Special Forces. Upon my return from Iraq in late 2003, my heart did not feel like it was missing something; it felt purpose. I trained for three years with Special

Forces following the invasion. I trained with the mindset that I would go back to Iraq in order to avenge the deaths of my brothers and to relieve whatever wildness my heart called so loudly for me to explore.

In my time with SF I trained for nearly a year as an Advanced Trauma Medic. Later I learned explosives and construction (yes, the two do go hand-in-hand) along with rigorous hours of hand–to-hand combat.

Patrolling and ambush techniques soon became second nature as I spent many long sleepless days and nights studying Small Unit Tactics. As training progressed, the instruction grew more complex and difficult because I was learning Persian culture and becoming familiar with the native language of Iran: Farsi.

A man by the name of Sam (whose last name I cannot disclose for security reasons) was my Persian teacher. As an Iranian native, Sam offered the class priceless knowledge on the depth of Persian culture. He would spend half the day teaching the basics of reading and writing Farsi and then spend the last few hours teaching in a story-type format.

The stories were where he would grab my attention, because they brought all lessons of the day into reality. From him I learned that the story of Conan the Barbarian came from a Persian hero by the name of Roostam. Sam always mentioned random facts that took me by surprise, such as the facts that windmills were created in Persia and that the bow and arrow was an old-style military tactic that

9

was used as advanced weaponry.

The most intriguing story for me, however, was of a man by the name of Hassanasaba. His name is where we get the modern day term assassin. This man trained over three hundred of Persia's elite who did not fear death and lived only for one single purpose and mission: to assassinate. I felt a personal connection to this story, because of the training I was taking.

I was being trained to be one of America's elite. No matter where I would go or what I would do, this story seemed to touch me in a way that made me see no limits in training and no mission too difficult.

My personal mission was to avenge the death of my friends from the invasion, and knowing this story made me believe that my mission was far from impossible. In time, the mission would be fulfilled.

I was surprised to find that most Iranians love Americans. Because their government has gone through many revolutions, the current regime does not like us at all. I was able to contrast this to the people of Iraq, who themselves love us and desire freedom and democracy. However, it is Iraq's government that has given its citizens a bad reputation. At the end of this training, I was put through a short survival school called Survival Evasion Resistance and Escape, or SERE.

I didn't quite make the cut in the end, and I was forced to pick a regular Army unit. I decided that with my training from the Marines, along with my Special Forces training and wartime experience, I was ready to go back to war. I was ready to avenge the death of my fallen brethren.

I sought out the first unit leaving and headed west to join them. Upon arrival at my new station in Fort Carson, Colorado Springs in July 2007, I was given the task to train eight men for six months prior to deployment. I thought this was a perfect opportunity to take men who had little experience and to give them everything I knew. I trained the men in hand-to-hand combat, advanced medical procedures, counter-terrorism techniques, and survival and evasion. One man out of this team was a big help. SGT Kevin Schafer from Batavia, Illinois was a hardened combat veteran and an ace with the M203 grenade launcher. With his help I was able to form an effective and lethal squad whose desire to fight and win was only second to the loyalty they held for each other.

One late Friday afternoon, the men were anticipating going home for the weekend. Everyone was outside waiting for word to be released for the weekend by the commander, when they began to grow restless.

Because we had trained for many long days in hand-to-hand combat, I told them that while we waited, we were all going to have some fun. I instructed them to get into two equal lines and put their backs to one another. Then they were instructed to all go to their knees.

When I gave the command "Go," they were all to turn around, face their competitor at once, and wrestle him to the ground, using the techniques I taught them. "Ready, set, go!" I shouted. No sooner did I shout the word "go" than all the men turned around and engaged in one huge brawl. Bodies were being flipped over, some were being locked in arm bars and screaming for mercy, and others laughed and messed with the weaker ones.

The brawl was a good way for the men to bond, to test what they had learned, and to relieve a bit of stress after a long workweek. A few minutes passed, I noticed some blood starting to spill among a few of the men. I smiled as I thought how this was going to bond them in a way that the protective Army would not have allowed in the past.

No sooner did I notice the blood than I heard, "Staff Sergeant Farina!" (Uh oh, it was the commander.) "What in the world are you doing out here with your men?"

"Well sir," I replied with a grin, "they're relieving a bit of stress after the workweek, and at the same time showing me what they've learned."

That didn't go over too well. I was ordered to cease the activity and not to let it happen again. In the Army there are some things a man can't experience until he gets to combat.

After months of training (which was controlled more after that particular Friday's exercise) our unit left the home we knew in Colorado and set out for Iraq. After being gone for four years, I ended up in the exact same place in Iraq as the first time around: *Baghdad.*

2

COP Ford

Life was not easy at COP Ford. The outpost was named in memory of Sergeant Ford, an experienced and veteran infantryman who was killed by an enemy sniper in 2007. Our outpost was located in a part of the Adhamiyah District of Baghdad. Located west of Sadr City, the neighborhood known as Beida was primarily inhabited by upper middle-class Iraqis who dealt in banking and medical services.

The sector we patrolled had a population that numbered between 150,000 and 225,000 Iraqis and was thought to be a place of low violence where we could make great strides in providing security and stability.

Adhamiyah was not plagued by high intensity conflict, but it was used by the local Mehdi Army militia as a ground for financing their operations through extortion of the markets, blackmail, and other petty crimes. We received minimal warning prior to our movement to this area of Baghdad. At the time, we had been operating in the Hussaniyah area north of Baghdad which was on the border of the Baghdad and Diyala Provinces.

Some men were excited and anxious to begin our mission in Baghdad while others felt a sense of intimidation, being so close to the bastion of anti-Americanism that was Sadr City. However, the recent cease-fire between the government and the Mehdi militia brought calm to the region, and though this gave them men hope for a peaceful deployment, tensions were still alive. The next fourteen months would be a test, but no one had a clue in what form the testing would come.

Upon arrival to COP Ford, our unit was informed it was used as a Ba'ath Party Youth recreation center (which was surrounded by the city). After an initial assessment, it was deemed top priority to give attention to the basic structure of our living conditions. One imminent issue was that an old generator that powered the outpost required constant attention. Its lack of maintenance was symptomatic of the entire installation.

The unit we replaced, members of the 82nd Airborne Division, had done very little to improve their surroundings and to ensure sustainability. Regardless of its state, we noted the building's vast potential and started repairing it at once. The generator would shut down, forcing all to sit in darkness for hours. Sometimes when a platoon would be out patrolling for hours, soldiers would look forward to coming home to a good meal and maybe a warm shower. Hopelessness ensued upon return, knowing the power was going to be out for the next day or two. We asked questions like: "How was it that the military could spend billions of dollars on this war but not provide the basics of life for its soldiers?" or "How was it that soldiers stationed elsewhere in such places as Kuwait or a mere twenty miles away could enjoy all sorts of luxuries?"

If someone was caught complaining about conditions at another base that had the comforts and simple things we longed for, he was silenced immediately. We had to make do with what little there was to offer, including hope. This is one of the leading factors of how a unit will bond and stand strong through the rigorous days in combat.

Daily life brought boredom, which forced the men to find ways to occupy the time. Some popular items were a deck of cards (which could go a long way), an educational magazine, or a book. The sense of futility in living the same day repeatedly would empower depression in the mind. A man could be happy one minute with his daily schedule.

Once the power would go out, however, the temperature would rise, and a pleasant moment of solace would turn into an eternity of sweat and frustration. The building would turn into an oven, making one wonder if the misery would ever come to an end.

If sitting in the darkness, sweating, and contemplating boredom did not make you think twice about the bad things you had done in your life, you had a hardened soul. Iraq and its surroundings had a way of exposing life's regrets. These were the times when I was made to be still and draw closer to the Lord.

I was alone with my thoughts for many hours, and they would keep me company as they had done in prior deployments. Prayer is where I would always find myself, because only these times are where I could overcome the major issues in my life that brought me pain and remorse. It appeared that the Lord waited for these times to come. Only then could I hear him speak.

One issue that brought the highest of highs and the lowest of lows was the food. The issues with our food started with the quality of refrigeration or the lack thereof. The refrigeration available was not enough to prevent the frozen goods from spoiling, which did happen at one point, leaving the men to scrounge. Grilled meat was the only source of food for about the first month, along with whatever packages families and friends would send. One of the best morale boosters on COP Ford was an old fifty-five gallon drum that had been cut in half, welded to a frame, and fashioned into a grill.

Always in use, the smell of charcoal and lighter fluid emanated from the courtyard of the building around the clock. At any time, day or night, the scents of burning wood and cooked meat with a hint of spices and sauces would greet your nostrils, enticing the pleasure receptors. The men enjoyed this ability to cook their food, because it was one of the few pleasures of living independently of supervision from Battalion headquarters. Nights after patrol could bring a moment of comfort as we enjoyed each other's company, reminiscent of a Sunday afternoon barbeque.

Good eating habits were essential to balance out the calories burnt as the missions in our sector got longer and the days grew hotter. This is why carbohydrates became a commodity: something hoarded and hidden from prying eyes and sticky fingers. There were a few places in our areas of responsibility where the soldiers on patrol could buy fresh bread that was baked in a brick oven.

Upon discovery, the bread was beyond compare. It tasted warm and soft, better than bread from home. The one thing I did learn about bread baked in a brick oven is that no bakery's product tastes the same as another's. This is because the yeast bakes into the walls of the brick oven, giving each bakery a distinct flavor that can't be replicated.

Our first sergeant put in a request for several Army cooks to help prepare our food. The request would take until the fifth month of our deployment, based on force protection issues, refrigeration, and the process of resupplying food and other goods. When the cooks arrived, our quality of life improved by receiving two meals a day:

balanced meals with options other than red meat. Looking forward to being able to eat twice a day seemed to be a luxury that was long forgotten. The cooks were an added bonus, because they were good-spirited individuals.

If someone came to chow a little late, this did not bother the cooks nor cause them to change how they served the patrol that had been out. They would get something ready and make sure the individual got a bite to eat. This one little act to bring the men food with no attitude raised the morale in this place. It brought the men one step closer to feeling normal.

One enjoyable moment through the summer was our Fourth of July feast, the first of its kind that the men enjoyed in half a year. The cooks, having planned early, were able to serve us a menu of ribs, steak, mashed potatoes, corn-on-the-cob, and an array of drinks. To finish off the evening, we were presented with a wide selection of desserts, ranging from fruit pies to cakes and other special treats.

One would think the unique thing about being in a war zone on the July 4th would be fireworks. However, there are many regulations and restrictions placed on the use of flares, star clusters, and other pyrotechnics that prohibited us from making our own fireworks show that night. With all of this, one could for a small time bring back the true meaning of the holiday.

Another issue was the sanitation services: showers and port-a-johns. For the first five months of the deployment, COP Ford would host between one hundred and one hundred fifty soldiers. But for a short time between late March and late May, the Army increased our capacity to over three hundred fifty soldiers. When the numbers were at one hundred fifty, the facilities were not enough. At twice that number, they became a major problem. This major sanitation issue during the Battle for Sadr City turned into a morale problem. When the battle peaked in April, the Iraqi men who came to empty the port-a-johns were almost too afraid to provide the service for fear of being killed because of their association with Americans. Eventually, a shower trailer was installed, and that eased tensions. But this only happened after the battle in Sadr City.

There was a time when a few friends became permanent residents of the COP: our dogs. Domino was purchased out in town as a young pup. He was a white dog with black spots that became quite ornery when someone would try to move him from his nice cool floor to the outside.

He did a good job of escorting the guard shifts from the inside of the building to the gate. He would always wait outside the sleeping bay for three men suited up in gear to walk out and call his name. Domino would proceed to follow them as they headed out to the entry gate, walking by their side without a care in the world.

The shift that was coming inside had Domino walk back with them, unless, of course, a stray cat or rat was in the immediate area. That was Domino's cue to go chase the animal away. He boosted morale by always being open for a good pat on the head. If someone was grilling food, he was there waiting for whatever morsel would be thrown his way.

Domino had two other companions with him at the COP when we arrived. One was a female dog whose type I don't know, but she was a golden, skinny dog. The other dog represented something of a shepherd. He was the father-figure and watchdog of the group.

A cat attempted to test our perimeter one night, and the shepherd caught onto its actions, chasing him out the main gate. The cat found a way to jump fifteen feet into the air to the nearest window ledge in fear of his life. These animals welcomed us back each day and made us remember that we were still human on those days that we didn't think we were or that we resembled much of anything. They were our companions in this war.

Regardless of our friendship with them, our higher-level command instructed us to get rid of the two small dogs but permitted us to keep the shepherd. They said the shepherd served a purpose, but the other two didn't. This affected a lot of men, because Domino had become part of the family. Regardless of how we felt as a group, the orders were carried out, and the two smaller dogs were dropped off in town.

Another friend of the area was a local Kurdish man who was a neighbor. He would always come out to the guard post at the entrance and talk to the men, making casual conversation. He often brought the men on guard small comfort items like tea, ice cream, cigarettes, or anything they requested. He strived to establish a good relationship with the soldiers from the beginning, because he was grateful for the security they provided his family. When the soldiers would offer the man money for comfort items, he would reply, "No thank you. God has blessed me with enough money; so I am happy to give some back."

Within a few months of our occupation of COP Ford, a few road issues came up because of the extreme abuse by our tracked vehicles. The edge of the Kurdish man's driveway was right in direct line of the outpost. As time wore on, holes in the road made it impossible for the man to leave his house using his own vehicle. It took two months to service the holes in the road that led out of COP Ford.

The Kurdish man never displayed anger, nor did he say a mean word to the soldiers because of these problems. In the end, COP Ford was fixed up better than anyone could have expected, thanks to the persistence of Company Commander Todd Looney, Executive Officer CPT Boyes, and First Sergeant Gonzales. They all played integral roles in getting the COP in great condition, a place many of us would come to know as not only a home but a refuge and place of memories.

New paint was added along with a new menu that let the cooks become more creative with their meals. The roads that led in and out of the COP were paved, and the landing zone received even better attention after two helicopters crashed onto it. Even our courtyard in the middle of the building received decking; it was an oasis for the men. It had a new barbecue grill pit constructed from sheets of metal by the maintenance men. It was a place to relax and forget for a moment where you were. The COP was an impressive place that saw us through the battles endured in this hell. It was a place the men would never forget as long as they lived.

3

The Price Paid
(February -March 2008)

3 ᴿᴰ brigade, 4th Infantry Division arrived in Iraq after Thanksgiving in the fall of 2007. The unit was located on a former Iraqi Air Force base that was north of Baghdad, known as Camp Taji. This is where all equipment was staged to include all items brought from Colorado along with equipment left by previous units such as vehicles, gear for searching houses, and identification systems that would be helpful in confirming wanted criminals. At Camp Taji units made final preparations with their men for combat operations by conducting rehearsal training of how to patrol and react to enemy fire. Charlie Company 1-6 lived there for about forty-five days before moving to Combat Outpost Ford (or COP Ford for short) in

Baghdad.

COP Ford was named after a soldier who gave his life in the War on Terror who died at the hands of an enemy sniper. We completed the transition process into COP Ford when our company was scheduled to receive new Humvees (the Army was replacing M1114s with new model M1151s). The M1151s were the new standard Humvee, and the Army was working on getting units in theater with these vehicles. One thing I liked about the new version was air conditioning, a luxury I thought wasn't possible in Iraq.

During the invasion of Iraq in 2003, the only air conditioning available was the natural kind: unzipping windows on the vehicles. Air conditioning was a small comfort that made life easier. The vehicles were modern in terms of technology, equipped with computer systems that would help with navigation and communication, which were crucial to mission accomplishment.

Once Charlie Company settled in, a rotation was set up so the three platoons could go back to Taji for the new vehicles. This gave the crews a break for a day: chances to get a haircut, eat in a real dining facility, and take a hot shower. It was here that the platoons would have to sign for the new vehicles and turn in the old ones.

First Lieutenant Galen Peterson's Blue Platoon (colors were used to designate the different platoons involved in a company or unit during operations) was told that he would be the first to get vehicles from Taji and would have an extra vehicle in his convoy. That vehicle would be the company commander's, and three men from the headquarters' platoon would man it. Lieutenant Peterson set out for camp Taji with his men, staying for the three days to get the old vehicles turned in and the new ones signed for.

After all the initial maintenance was conducted and the vehicles prepped, Peterson was ready to make the trip back to COP Ford. On these trips, men had to be on guard, watching the area for anything suspicious. Someone always had a story about his family or the latest news. The long trips from one base to another provided opportunity to crack a good joke and start the major trash talking about one another which always seemed to bond men in the military.

Peterson's convoy was traveling along a major road from Taji to Ford, which in America would seem like four lanes but in Iraq was only three. The third vehicle of the five-vehicle convoy was the commander's. This vehicle carried Staff Sergeant Michael Elledge as the truck commander, Sergeant Christopher Simpson as the vehicle's gunner sitting in the turret of the vehicle, and Specialist Keith Hanson as the vehicle's driver for the trip.

Out of all the men, Sergeant Simpson was closest to the company commander, Captain Todd Looney. He had been the commander's driver for two years, a time during which they bonded. SSG Elledge was the usual gunner, but in this particular instance the crew switched duties. Simpson was not only the commander's driver, but anytime the commander would get out of his vehicle to check on a situation, Simpson was always right there by his side as his personal security officer. For the longest time, the commander would view these three as family. This bond was created because the Army would have them spending more time together than they did with their own families.

Approximately 20 minutes into the trip, the headquarters' vehicle passed a line of HESCO baskets on the side of the road. To give you an idea, a HESCO basket is made up of rough, durable material, surrounded in basket form by a metallic fencing and then filled with dirt. These are lined up on major routes to prevent sniper fire, as well as making it more difficult for the enemy to plant an Improvised Explosive Device, sometimes called an IED or roadside bomb.

As the vehicles were passing the row of HESCOs, the headquarters' vehicle was about halfway through the row of baskets when an IED went off. Immediately the air filled with smoke, dirt, fire, and debris, making communication and visibility nearly impossible. The men in the rest of the vehicles came to a state of heightened alert in preparation for a secondary attack or an ambush which usually follows an IED strike.

Sergeant First Class Weatherly was in the vehicle behind Staff Sergeant Elledge when the explosion happened. Weatherly knew that communication lines had been severed, so his only hope to communicate with the vehicle that received damage was to get on his vehicle's loud speaker. He tried to make his voice heard by SGT Keith Hanson, who was driving the damaged vehicle. Following the strike, Hanson was shocked, confused, and angry all at once, making it difficult for him to understand what happened.

After regaining a sense of clarity, SGT Hanson followed SFC Weatherly's instructions of putting the vehicle in neutral so that he could be pushed through the blast zone and out of harm's way. LT Peterson commanded the rest of the vehicles to move about 150 meters down the road in the direction of travel to establish a cordon and to get a better assessment of the situation. LT Peterson's men were already on the radio, requesting medical evacuation and an Explosive Ordnance Disposal (EOD) team.

When everyone set up at the cordon, which is where you emplace security all around an area, the worst had been realized: Sergeant Christopher Simpson and Staff Sergeant Michael Elledge had given the ultimate sacrifice. They had gone home.

Of all days for this to happen, it was March 17th, St. Patrick's Day, a day dedicated to the feast of St. Patrick, the name of the feast presenting irony with the departed. The second hardest part about this day for the men was the waiting. They had to wait on site for five hours or more with the bodies of their brothers, which included Hanson, who had been right there with them through it all.

SGT Hanson was not among the deceased; however, his soul had taken such torment during this time that he could do nothing but process all the emotions this hit dealt. They had to wait at that location for assessment teams, medical teams, and an EOD team to arrive to do their work. Five hours passed until the night ended back at COP Ford, which felt like nothing short of an eternity.

During this time a series of feelings and emotions can seize a soldier: shock, transition to anger, and then to shock again. Hunger might be present, but little attention is given to basic needs like drinking water. These needs are ignored because the emotion of losing someone takes over every basic feeling. You feel so vulnerable to life and death because this type of event is something you can't prepare for. It's not like you can wake up one day and say, "Okay, today will be the day so-and-so dies. Now, I'm going to prepare myself mentally for it so I can remember to eat, drink water, and sleep when my body needs it."

You ignore all those feelings and focus on the core emotions of life. You focus on the loss you took, and then you focus on how you are going to settle the score. I remember having many talks with Simpson, often sharing the same point of view about the great luxurious lifestyle the Army had given us at COP Ford. Ford was a place that would make the worst slums in America feel like heaven. Simpson was a lighthearted man who, like me, could find humor in almost anything.

I could relate to Michael Elledge because he was a former Marine. He had taken the same path as I and left the Marines to find something better in the Army. Even though I didn't know him, he was still considered my brother. His being a Marine gave him that right, because in the Marines you come to find that once you're a Marine you're always a Marine. Everyone who endures time on Parris Island or in the Corps will always be your brother in some way. That's the way Marines are.

When the day ended, the bodies were sent off to processing and then flown home to their respective families. The Hero Flight is the name given to fallen service members during wartime. This would be the final flight home for Chris Simpson and Michael Elledge. The damaged vehicles would be brought back to COP Ford, where SSG Danny Bowden would be responsible for assessing the damage. He would have to determine what equipment would still be of value to the Army and in what way the equipment could help complete future missions. One of the most difficult tasks for anyone in the theater of operations is taking your job seriously, hours after losing someone close to you, and then looking at the place where the souls of those men left their bodies.

Specialist Nalls was selected to attend the funeral service for Staff Sergeant Michael Elledge, who was from Dearborn, Michigan. Nalls would face the family and the tears that came so naturally from such a great loss. He would help bring closure for the families involved. Michael's wife, Carleen, wanted to know what his last words were before he went home to the Lord. Those words, however, are reserved for her in due time.

At the service, people talked about how Michael was a happy guy who was full of life and God-fearing. At COP Ford he started a Bible study that helped people understand Christ better and bring the lost into the light. He always wanted to bring an unbeliever to Christ; that was his goal above all else.

The support after the funeral was something out of a movie. The streets of his home were lined with flags in honor of his service. After the ceremony, the Patriot Riders asked to escort the body, but the hearse-master showed up and asked to do the honors. He had a horse-driven wagon and charged $1,000 an hour, but he offered this honor for free.

Out of all the things that happened that day, the most coincidental of all would have to be the driver's name. It was Tommy Elledge. Tommy had no relation to Michael and was allowed to do the honors while the Patriot Riders followed right behind him.

People were on the sides of the street saluting or covering their hands over their hearts. Each overpass had firefighters and police who saluted as the hearse went by. At the burial site Taps was played, and full military honors were given. Under a tree on a hill in Westwood Hills Memorial Park in Placerville, California is where Michael's final resting place is. This is where he will wait in heaven for his wife Carleen.

In Syracuse, New York another branch of Team Steel's extended family had their day of mourning. Christopher Simpson's parents were the first to learn about the tragedy. Word of his death spread throughout the immediate family until it reached Carol Fries, Chris' fianceé. She was notified on the phone by Simpson's brother, Rich. Her thoughts came to a halt. Like getting kicked in the chest or falling to the ground and having the air knocked out of you... that's the only description that came close to the great pain she felt. How did this happen? Was the information that was being passed along a reality? Or was this one of those bad dreams from which you cannot awaken? Simpson's parents, his siblings, and his fianceé shared a profound sense of loss.

However, the love you have for a family member is somehow different from the feelings you have for a true love. Christopher was Carol's true love in life whom she had known since the age of fourteen. Now he was gone. How do you begin to cope with everyday essentials when something as life changing as this happens in an instant?

Pride.

Pride was the answer, because in her healing she found a pride for him that she had never felt for anyone else. In the days to come she would stick close to his family, as they would to her. This brought each of them strength. When Simpson's body landed on the runway of an airport near his home, you could see nothing but people waving

31

flags. Complete strangers, but patriots nonetheless, were among the huge crowd. Eight fire trucks escorted Chris Simpson's body through a flag-lined route, sounding off their loud sirens in respect for a fallen hero, as was done for Michael Elledge. The two equally received a hero's welcome home to their final resting places. While in the car following the body of her true love, Carol looked out the window at the overwhelming support and spotted two individuals who still make her cry to this day.

An older man was standing on the side of the road, holding the hand of a little boy who could have been no more than three. The boy was waving a flag, and the man was sobbing. He was sobbing for the death of a fallen hero who he respected but never got the chance to know. This man on the side of the road represented so many of us here in America. What we feel when a soldier returns home in this manner cannot be expressed in words. Behind all of this was a line of cars, two miles in length, flashing their lights and being as patriotic as they could.

All the support was overwhelming, as was the line for the viewing of Christopher in church. In the freezing cold for six to seven hours on that day people waited in line to see a hero. As it happened in Michael's funeral, they wanted to pay respects to a man who had given his life for their protection and freedom.

The weather didn't stop people, nor did the wait discourage them in their common cause of respecting the fallen. The hatred of the terrorist was not and will never be strong enough to break the bond of true love that Carol has for Christopher. If anything, it has only made the bond stronger, for she takes comfort in knowing that one day she will see him again. She will hold his face in her hands, and she will kiss him. In that moment all the pain she has felt and will feel in the future will cease for all time. The loss of these men, though tragic, served a purpose for the coming days of fighting. The memory of these two became a force that drove the men of Charlie Company to press on in battle when we needed strength the most.

For me, this was like reliving a nightmare of the invasion. In the invasion, everything started out calmly, and then the bombing that took four friends happened, followed by firefights for weeks ahead. All of the missions ended us up in Baghdad again. What was it about Baghdad that meant I must endure repetitive times of fighting and the loss of friends to this one area in the world?

That took me years to figure out. At the time of this writing it is 2013: five years after everything took place in Sadr City and four years after the first edition of this book. I figured out that there is a master plan for everyone. Even though you lose friends and witness horrible things in life, you must take heart in knowing that there is a grand design in play. Christ above has something in store for every person: a plan too great to fathom.

Faith is what has seen many men and women through battle. Faith is what has seen me through the darkest

33

times of my life. Faith is the same substance that carries people like Carol, Kate (Chris Simpson's mother), and Carleen through life. Faith is the only way to communicate with God. The stronger the faith, the better the communication. The power of faith is often underestimated. If we choose to have it, Christ will choose to show us the plan he has for us.

4

THE BATTLE FOR ROUTE GOLD
(Day 1: March 23, 2008)

SOON after the deaths of our brothers, Charlie Company was tasked to support Iraqi Army forces at a nearby checkpoint. Upon turning down the road where the checkpoint was emplaced, we saw a wall of concrete barriers ten feet high by four feet wide, interlocking with each other as they lined the road for miles. The barriers provided protection and created a control-point for vehicles that would pass through our area from Sadr City. Behind the walls on both sides was a labyrinth of one and two-story houses along with multiple apartment complexes. All of these houses were made of a brick and clay material that drank in the sun during the middle of the day and radiated heat onto any living thing nearby at dusk.

The checkpoint was in the center of the road with a guard tower that was high enough in the air to monitor approaching traffic. Thirty Iraqi Army soldiers led by an Iraqi colonel manned the checkpoint, equipped with one armored vehicle called a BMP, a Russian-made vehicle and a valuable weapon with the ability of its main gun to eliminate a large group of men in seconds. I was glad they were on our side and not the insurgency's. Soldiers at the checkpoint started receiving PSAF from buildings located perpendicular to friendly positions along Route Gold which ran north. Our soldiers were sent to evaluate the problem and, if necessary, to engage and destroy the enemy.

Peterson's platoon was called out to go to the Iraqi Army checkpoint on Route Gold. The other checkpoints in Sadr City, which were key checkpoints, had been over-run. Prior to the attack, the other four checkpoints in the city leading up to our area had been attacked so severely that they had been abandoned by the IA. The militia was determined to take this checkpoint, because it would allow them to place their forces throughout Baghdad and strike at U.S. forces whenever they wished. They attacked the previous checkpoints one after another and began to gain a foothold on our area. Charlie Company 1-68 along with 1-2 SCR's Bravo and Charlie Company's and various other units like Delta Company 4-64 and 3rd ID were the last line of defense for the fate of Baghdad.

As soon as Blue Platoon's four gun trucks appeared on site, they started taking enemy contact from the apartment complexes across the road. Each gun-truck picked a sector of fire and engaged. Truck commanders spotted targets and quickly notified other leaders in the area about the situation. The next vehicle would pick up an interlocking sector of fire with whatever vehicle would be close by.

When you coordinate interlocking sectors of fire, you need to make sure you are covering one hundred percent of a given area at all times. All the while, neither the insurgents nor the American soldiers were willing to give any ground to the other in this fight. The insurgents wanted this checkpoint because it determined victory for them and a defeat for the Americans, thus dealing a psychological blow to all American forces in Baghdad.

If the enemy had taken this particular checkpoint, the battle would have been longer and bloodier than it was in reality. Peterson's men had to hold this ground because it was a strategic position when it came to defending our area of Baghdad. Also, it became a place where we could meet up with terrorism and do our jobs as soldiers: eliminating the enemy wherever they may want to fight. If all failed to keep this ground, much hope and many lives could be lost. However, if by some chance we could defeat the vast numbers of insurgents who had already been successful in taking four other checkpoints, we would be well on our way to winning the fight for Baghdad. In addition, we would gain the loyalty and trust of the people in the neighborhood we protected. As you can see, there was a lot at stake here besides a person's own life: there were a community of Iraqis and our own country that depended on us to defend this ground with our lives.

So we fought.

Peterson was on the ground, evaluating the situation with an Iraqi Army colonel. The firing increased, and an RPG flew straight overhead into one of the IA guard towers. Those within a twenty-meter radius of the building could feel the concussion of the impact. A thick cloud of brown smoke erupted from the two-man tower. Blue Platoon reinforced the Iraqi Army checkpoint on Gold while the checkpoint was under coordinated attack. Immediately upon arriving at the checkpoint, all vehicles came under heavy DSHKA, PKC, and small arms fire from dominating buildings in multiple directions. The platoon received additional RPG fire from the apartment complex to the northeast. All vehicles returned fire with small arms and crew-served weapons. Lieutenant Peterson, Sergeant Edwin, Specialist Cory Bushell, Private First Class Nicholas Monks, and Linguist "Z" positioned themselves northeast of the checkpoint, facing the apartment buildings.

Edwin immediately used his M240B machine gun to suppress enemy positions in the apartment complex that were within 100 meters. His method was controlled and accurate. Only firing a few rounds with each squeeze of the trigger, he maintained ammunition discipline so he would not run out too early in the fight. Aiming through his weapon, he found a group of insurgents and fired upon them. Scan, aim, and fire again was his method until the immediate threat was neutralized. Edwin's only cover from enemy fire would be a little bit of camouflage and a series of metallic plates that could stop small arms fire.

Edwin engaged the enemy RPG team with a series of short controlled bursts as it maneuvered through the upper floors of the apartment buildings, preventing it from getting a good top-down shot at Blue Platoon positions. Edwin coordinated with the other vehicles to ensure that ammunition reloads were continuous and sustained so onslaught on the enemy would prove effective.

Communication was difficult because he had to get on the radio to make sure all units were on the same sheet of music when they were given instructions. The vehicle radios always had a loudspeaker attached so they could be heard easily over gunfire in the background. He basically put out a series of commands, and someone from each vehicle acknowledged what was ordered and followed through on the assignment. Cross talking was useful because it was quick and effective communication to deliver a command that was needed.

Bushell dismounted to protect the dead spaces (places that can't be seen due to cover) near Peterson's truck. He engaged the enemy with M4 rifle fire while the crew-served weapons were reloading and helped ensure there was enough water for the men in the vehicles who were engaging the enemy. Bushell continued to engage the enemy despite the heavy small arms fire directed against him from two directions and an RPG that detonated on the tower above him. He did not mind one bit all the debris that fell from the tower as a result of the rocket's impact. The smoke obscured his vision and made it hard to breathe, but Bushell knew he had to keep firing. Monks maneuvered the truck to allow Edwin the best field of fire against the constantly moving enemy while using the scant cover to protect the truck from RPGs.

Staff Sergeant David Rocha, Sergeant Kyle Kincaid, and Private First Class Derek Quinn set in position northeast of the checkpoint, facing the apartment buildings. Rocha was driving in order to continue commanding his vehicle while still providing another dismount to the fight. He then communicated with the adjacent vehicles to maneuver on the RPG team on the south end of the apartment complex, as well as to coordinate ammunition reloads. Kincaid dismounted to help protect the flanks of his vehicle and to provide covering fire while the crew-served weapons were reloading. Quinn suppressed the RPG team in the alleys, denying them a clear keyhole shot at the platoon. He was quickly running out of places to use as cover from the incoming fire in all directions. Despite an RPG detonating in front of Edwin's vehicle and heavy small arms fire coming from two directions,

Quinn continued to return fire.

Staff Sergeant Danny Key, Sergeant Juan Perez, Specialist Daniel Garcia, and Private First Class Billy Bailey set in position northwest of the checkpoint, guarding the north flank of the platoon. Key selected a position between one of the massive barriers and the main checkpoint that afforded his truck excellent cover while maintaining wide fields of fire.

As the enemy maneuvered through the apartment buildings, Key sent communication using the vehicle's radio system with the other trucks to track the movements of enemy combatants. Perez suppressed enemy positions in the apartment complex, preventing the enemy from maneuvering on the north flank of the platoon. Garcia used his M249 squad automatic weapon to provide extra firepower against the insurgents when they attempted to maneuver to the north by running on foot from their initial attack position.

Weatherly's crew set in position controlling the Gold and Grizzlies intersection. Butler courageously fired from his M240 machine gun to suppress the DSHKA, forcing the enemy to break contact. The men who manned the DSHKA left the gun in place and ran for their lives. The insurgents thought they could fire a few shots and make Butler run; however, they ended up having a bad teatime and took off to their mommies!

Butler then shifted fire to the PKC, helping force the enemy firing from it to break contact as well. These guys ran to join the other crew who had the bad teatime and found their mommies as well. I suspect that group of insurgents all had a good cry that night. He continued to suppress enemy positions without regard to the RPG that barely missed his HMMV turret, exploding on the concrete wall next to him. Weatherly immediately began pushing information to Captain Looney and cross-talking with Red Platoon, which was spinning up to reinforce.

As soon as Air Weapons Teams came on the net, Weatherly directed them to observe the enemy's rear to deny them the ability to maneuver through the apartment complex. Wallis maneuvered the truck in a series of survivability moves, disrupting the enemy's efforts to place massive fires upon the vehicle. Additionally, Wallis helped scan the traffic circle, acquiring and positively identifying targets for Butler to engage. Sergeant Williams protected the south flank of the platoon and continued to handle ammunition for Butler, allowing him to maintain rapid and sustained fire upon the enemy. The actions of Weatherly's men forced the enemy crew- served weapons (PKC, DSHKA) to break contact, helping to prevent the platoon from taking casualties.

Soon the day drew to a close, and the men headed back to the outpost to regroup and to figure out exactly what had happened at the checkpoint. Many more days lay ahead for this crew. Today was only a small taste of what was to come. When the men came back that night, you could see the sense of pride on all of their faces for having fought such a battle. For most of them it was the first time they had ever fired a live round in the direction of another human. The chatter went on into the early hours of the morning as the men relived the battle. In other rooms at our outpost you could hear a lot of laughter as the men were in high spirits. They would definitely need this for the days of fighting to come.

(Day 2: March 24, 2008)

Gold Platoon, AKA the Beavers, showed up on the scene in the morning of March 24, and First Lieutenant Jeffery Nelson, the Platoon Leader for the Beavers, was on the ground with the interpreter, "Tank." They began talking with the same Iraqi Army colonel who was with us the day before. Tank was given his name by our platoon due to security reasons. He couldn't walk around Baghdad expecting to be safe if his full name were on his uniform. He also had to wear a face-mask. If an insurgent found out he was working with us, Tank's whole family could have been jeopardized. We gave him that name because he was built like a tank, 280 pounds of sheer muscle and attitude.

Nelson was evaluating the situation when gunfire broke out. Having only minimal troops on the ground, he requested the rest of my squad to help support. I and my trusted team leader and friend, Kevin Schafer, were ordered to dismount along with the rest of my squad. We

43

were to link up with Nelson on the ground to gain an over-watch position and return fire on any threats that our four vehicles could not engage. Suddenly, gunshots rang out from all directions. The men immediately hunkered down to covered positions in search of whoever was firing while I searched for a route to get the men to a stable position and repel our attackers.

I maneuvered my men to a location near a mosque located behind a wall that separated the street from the neighborhood. Schafer and I devised a quick plan of getting into a nearby building that could overlook the area from where the gunfire was coming. Approximately 100 meters across the road, a group of apartment complexes was being used as a hideout for the JAM. The JAM is the Jash-Al-Mahdi or the Mahdi Army. They were roughly 60,000 strong and possessed hardened loyalties to Muslim Shiite cleric Muqtada Al Sadr.

My squad began maneuvering through a few alleyways in the labyrinth of the city. Schafer, my alpha team leader, had a round impact above his head, coming within mere inches of hitting him. We knew we were getting close to something bigger at this point, which meant we had to keep pressing harder to an elevated position. As we came around the corner of one street, LT Johnson located a suitable building where we could take up an over-watch position of the area from where we were receiving contact. This elevated position gave us a strategic advantage in the fight. I ordered Schafer to breach a door to a small house to gain access into an adjacent building.

The rest of the squad followed while pulling security on all angles. Once on the roof, we immediately took fire from multiple directions. Men were firing at us to our direct front, using multiple balconies and rooftops. Some of our attackers were coming from Iraqi Army positions on the ground and in other buildings where friendly Iraqis were supposed to be. I ordered my squad to immediately return fire once they identified a hostile target.

I had to emplace four men of the Bravo team along with Lieutenant Nelson on the right side of the roof while Schafer's team and I took up the left side of the roof. On the left side, we found a large satellite dish and a few scattered metal chairs we could use for cover. We had to be careful to avoid shooting in random directions because we had friendly forces on the ground along with innocent civilians in the houses nearby. All soldiers knew from the beginning of combat operations that if they were to shoot a civilian, the people we are trying to protect, the mission could be jeopardized. It would also give the insurgency, who were sworn to kill all Americans, a psychological advantage in the war.

Both teams began engaging targets simultaneously as enemy gunmen attempted to engage us from not only the rooftops and balconies, but from the streets and alleyways down below as well. The shootings would start and last for a few minutes and then stop, only to start again: a continuous cycle of firing and silence. This went on for about 20 minutes. When all fighting had stopped for some time, I called a ceasefire. We exited the building to set up security positions on the ground and to gain hold of possible avenues of enemy approach so we could engage more effectively if necessary.

Heading down the multiple flights of stairs and through the building, my men seemed to move in groups of two without having to be told. Each soldier automatically paired up with another and moved while providing cover. We moved quickly yet cautiously through the building and exited into the streets where the firing had begun but was now silent. A movement like this with a small element to ensure security and a neutralized threat could take longer than twenty minutes, but it seemed like only five.

Our minds were engaged at this point in staying alive and keeping our heightened senses clear so that we could zero in on any threats that were left over. Neither the heat nor the dryness in our mouths mattered while we moved to another location after the initial attack, because all we could think about was survival and getting home alive.

Later we discovered that some of the Iraqi Army and Iraqi Police were two-sided. The insurgents paid off certain Iraqi civilians and promised them protection if they would wear a uniform of the Iraqi Police or Iraqi Army. When the time came to fight, we could see these men looking directly at us while engaging with their weapons with the intent to kill, not harass. You can always tell an enemy's intent in battle if you can catch a glimpse of his eyes. When an individual intends to harass you in combat, his eyes are wide open with a blank look, and the emotion of fright is written across his face. The eyes of a killer, however, are sharp. His stance and body position are straight, and he does not waver or lose his guard due to fear. These Iraqis worked against us, which made this type of warfare most deadly and confusing.

The vehicles on the ground were suppressing the enemy with precision gunfire on locations that would be called in from our over-watch position. The insurgents fired from all directions, including from a power plant near a building from where we had been fired upon earlier. Occupying and firing from the power plant was a brilliant strategy on the insurgents' part. The insurgents knew we could not suppress them unless we destroyed the power plant. They also knew we would be hesitant to do so, as some 100,000 residents would lose power as a result, potentially causing a civilian uprising. So our soldiers guided the vehicles to start suppressing in other directions from where we had seen the enemy as well as from new enemy positions.

Once my squad was out of the building and back on the ground, everything seemed so quiet that I was asked to escort the interpreter inside the mosque for some water. As we came out, I was told that upon entering a sniper had put two rounds above my head, impacting within one foot and shattering glass on the ground. I did not

47

believe what happened, but when I looked up I saw the bullet holes and broken glass in the entrance right where I had been moments ago.

This was the first of many times I entertained the thought that angels actually watched over all of us on the ground. I held tightly to prayer and my rosary for many days after this incident. I remember calling out more frequently for protection from our Lord as the days of heavy fighting would increase. Protection is what I asked for, and protection is exactly what the Lord gave me.

(Day 3: March 25, 2008)

Upon heading out the following day, which was the second day for our platoon and the third total day of the engagement, we had taken one more vehicle than usual. On this particular day, I brought along from my squad Private Raymond Blake, who would be at my side on the ground, as well as Specialist Cedrick Bryant, who would be driving the vehicle. My Bravo Team leader, Sergeant Floyd Payne, grabbed the gunner position, and Specialist Louis Medina was my automatic rifleman. Everyone from my squad seemed to want to get in on the action after day one, so I took who I could.

SFC Ullrich, the platoon sergeant, ordered Staff Sergeant Lewis, the second squad leader, to bring his men while I accompanied them to clear a route in the area, a mission that was only supposed to take a little over an hour. We were only supposed to stop and talk for a few minutes to the Iraqi Army colonel, the same one from two days prior who was in charge of Iraqi forces on the ground. Upon reaching the checkpoint, it was only a matter of minutes before we came under heavy gunfire from the same locations as the day before.

Lewis maneuvered his men into a two-story building, leaving two riflemen on the ground for security. I decided it would be best to stay with the men outside should something go wrong. Specialist Christopher Fox grabbed the M-14 sniper rifle from the vehicles and headed to the stairwell on the rooftop of the building. Private Michael Ervin was placed at the bottom of the building for security, and the rest were on the second floor, reinforcing positions and taking cover. We anticipated a large-scale confrontation.

These men were better trained than most infantrymen, as they required little leadership in such situations. They knew exactly what to do, and when given the order to return fire they did so in a disciplined manner, firing only at confirmed targets. Lewis began to fortify the rooms in the building he controlled. It was a three-story apartment building with an access door to the roof. The roof provided an excellent field of view and a direct line of sight but did not offer much in terms of protection.

As Lewis and his men were in the building, I stayed outside with Medina and Blake to keep an eye on the Iraqi soldiers in case there was an attack from the ground. We were the extra set of eyes for the men in the building. After a half hour, a mortar round struck the ground near our location, wounding an Iraqi Army soldier. Upon seeing this, I called on the radio for guidance and was instructed to head into the building.

To me, mortar fire meant that the other men and I on the ground had been in the same place too long and that it was time to move. The enemy was zeroing in on our position, and we could only guess where the next round would land. I quickly guided Blake and Medina to the building where Lewis had established a defensive position. Ervin signaled us to the doorway and provided cover during our movement into the building.

Once in the building, I gave Blake and Medina guidance on areas that should be watched and mentioned only a few words about our ROE (Rules of Engagement) as a reminder of who and what to engage. After about ten minutes in the building, the gunshots from the opposing location started, and within moments greatly increased. At first Blake and Sergeant Patrick Simpson, Lewis's Bravo Team leader, took turns scanning for immediate threats of insurgents across the road. They positioned themselves on a balcony adjacent to rooms where the other men were positioned.

As they were scanning, Blake felt the impact of a round directly next to his head, which motivated Blake to come inside the building. Fox could be heard identifying various targets and engaging them with great accuracy. As the fire increased, Lewis added more men to the balcony in order to have more eyes on the area of threat. Lewis was not the kind to step up with his men. Rather, he would lead from the rear, from the back of the room. His philosophy was that if he was shot, no one could take his place; so above all, he had to ensure his own safety.

This is one of many characteristics that separated myself from this timid leader. You have to be right at the side of your men during the worst of it in order to gain their respect and loyalty. Private Coung Nguyen was instructed to break out a nearby window and move a couch to his location to provide a steady platform from which to fire and also to use as cover.

Nguyen noticed that our tracer rounds were impacting certain windows of a third story building. A moment later, a whiz came by his head—likely from a room on the third story of the same building. As soon as this happened, Sergeant First Class Ullrich ordered every man to suppress the threat area to provide fire superiority.

"Move! Move! Everyone get behind some cover and start giving these bastards hell!" Ullrich shouted. "If anyone spots someone on the other side of the street with a gun, waste them ... no questions asked!" His voice was stern and loud enough to be heard clearly over the incoming rounds that were ricocheting all around the multiple rooms we were in. So many bullets came our way, but not once did any man give way to the position that was being held.

51

After this, there was about a half an hour of silence. So I went to the window to scan the area for anyone who might be brave enough to still fight. I could not see anyone immediately, though looking through your sight and breathing heavily from such an adrenaline rush will at times make concentration a bit difficult.

Our first firefight must have gone on for fifteen plus minutes until there was a break in the action. Kneeling on the balcony for only a few minutes, two rounds smacked the wall directly above my head and to the left of my face. I remember shouting something like, "That's four!"

In the background, Lewis shouted back, "What's four? What are you talking about?"

"That makes four rounds in two days to hit right above my head. Jesus must really think I am way too pretty to get a scratch on my face!"

In the middle of fighting, I always thought it necessary to break the tension and crack some kind of a joke. It actually helped me focus. Simpson took aim next and fired two rounds from his grenade launcher, impacting some 100 meters away in a third-story room of an apartment complex from which we were taking fire. When I was shot at, he had noticed muzzle flashes from a specific room and immediately engaged. Simpson never felt the need to waste time and call up a threat when he knew one was obviously there. He locked on the target and engaged them with aggression and accuracy: a deadly combination. Simultaneously, I heard Fox on the rooftop firing every few seconds with his sniper rifle. He spotted enemies not only at the same window Simpson did but also on the rooftop of the building. Some of the gunmen were using satellite dishes as cover, while others were using water tanks on the roof.

Fox had his hands full; so all who were in the building began engaging the same target areas once we received word from Fox what was happening. SFC Ullrich had enough at this point as well; so he busted out a window and began engaging. There was something in his method of firing that I noticed: it was calm, effective, rapid, and destructive. He would reload with great finesse, all the while keeping his eyes on the targets and never on his weapon.

I don't know what was going on in his head at that moment when I noticed all of this. It could have been that he was protecting his men, or perhaps he was mad at terrorism in general. It was possible that he was unleashing anger about being over here in the war for a third time. In the end, the reasons for his intensity did not matter. What mattered was that he stood strong as a leader in the presence of his men and in the face of the enemy.

No sooner had I reloaded my weapon then an RPG hit directly below Simpson and me on the floor of the balcony. I fell back from the concussion of the blast and cursed everything, saying that summer camp was not worth $5.50 an hour and that I was not going back out on the window. After Blake and I finished having our pity party,

Blake took up a secure position, and I headed back out to the balcony. Nguyen immediately engaged targets in another one of the apartment buildings, suppressing with a fierce accuracy that brought death to our attackers.

As Simpson engaged targets with his M203 once again, Lewis, the rest of the men, and I returned fire from the windows in adjacent rooms and from the balcony itself. Fox was heard once more unleashing hell with his precision weapon. CRACK! CRACK! CRACK! That was the only sound coming from Fox's direction with an occasional, "Yeah, how do you like that, baby?" or "Woohoo!" I think the dear old lad was having way too much fun at this time. However, he did his job exceptionally well.

Meanwhile, on the ground another battle was taking place with the vehicles that were firing at targets on the streets and in alleyways. Bryant and Sergeant Payne were in one vehicle while Payne received guidance over the radio to locate the fire. Payne started firing at the same location everyone else was. Rounds hit in front of the driver's side mirror and on top of the window of his vehicle.

Private First Class Walter Lopez got out of his vehicle so that his gunner, Corporal Gary Muckelvaney, could pull security one way and get eyes on another direction down Route Gold. He wanted to be out on the ground and not stuck in a vehicle because his other brothers were already in the fight. His timing was advantageous, because an RPG then blew up twenty meters from him on the barrier wall. With the direction Lopez was now facing, he was able to spot the insurgent responsible. He opened fire with nearly a full magazine, first out of fear and then anger, all the while shouting, "This is how me and my peeps do it in the OC!" He made the insurgents think twice about confronting this little feisty Mexican again.

Our platoon fought for another five hours until Blue Platoon showed up as a relief in place. The arrival of Blue Platoon at the checkpoint allowed all of us, the mighty "Beaver Platoon," a much-needed opportunity to head back to COP Ford for resupply. At the time of their arrival, the checkpoint was under sporadic small arms fire. So Blue Platoon talked with the IA commanders at the checkpoint to get them to clear the apartment complex to the northeast.

The IA said they had observed and engaged enemy fighters emplacing IEDs and booby traps throughout the apartment complex. Our battalion had received tips about IEDs and EFPs along the routes approaching the checkpoint, warning all units to maneuver with caution.

Additionally, AWT had observed 70 to 100 individuals inside the apartment complex preparing for an attack, but the AWT had to break station to refit. Captain Looney ordered Blue Platoon, which was led by Lieutenant Peterson, to check on security checkpoints and deter enemy attack against them. Blue Platoon was at an SOI checkpoint about a half a mile away, observing the enemy attack the IA checkpoint. Upon witnessing the attack, the platoon moved to help the Iraqi Army at the checkpoint.

The platoon came under small arms fire from the slums north of the checkpoint and returned precision 5.56 mm fire against 2 military-aged men with AK-47s.

The sounds of battle around the IA checkpoint increased, and thus more fighting began. IA platoons in Humvees and armored cars were moving back and forth on Route Gold, moving to and from the checkpoint. Suddenly, while en route, an IA patrol stopped Blue Platoon to ask for assistance with two WIAs. Private First Class Levitan, the platoon medic, and Sergeant Kincaid helped render aid to the WIA. They were able to stabilize one of the WIAs, but the other died of wounds at 2 p.m., a few hours later. The IA patrol leader reported that the Route Gold IA checkpoint was taking heavy casualties and the enemy attack was overrunning them. Blue Platoon counterattacked down Route Gold towards the IA checkpoint. About 600 meters from the checkpoint, the platoon began to take small arms fire from both sides of the road.

Peterson's men observed RPGs impacting on IA vehicles, causing at least one IA Humvee to catch fire. Staff Sergeant Rocha observed numerous explosions throughout the entire checkpoint, which the IA later reported as the beginning of a mortar attack that lasted until Blue Platoon's counterattack reached the barrier obstacles. Heavy small arms fire escalated at the checkpoint and the platoon began to take RPG and heavy small arms fire 400 meters from the checkpoint. A platoon of IA armored cars passed through Blue Platoon at a high rate of speed, firing in all directions. IA Ford trucks and Humvees were evacuating casualties through Blue Platoon's axis of advance. Upon arriving at the north end of the checkpoint barriers, Blue Platoon found the IA infantry pinned down behind the western barriers.

Three IA armored cars continued to maneuver at high speed through the street, placing sporadic fire in all directions regardless of friendly positions and nearly running over several soldiers on the ground. Shortly after this incident, all five of the Iraqi heavy-armored vehicles were silent and appeared disabled. None of the IA vehicles were placing crew-served fire upon the enemy. It was clear that Blue Platoon would be on its own as it counterattacked and that time was critical.

Later, about seven enemy combatants broke through to the west side of the checkpoint near the mosque (the one that had taken an RPG earlier the day prior) and placed fire on the IA pinned down in the storefront area. The Blue Platoon trucks established a support by fire position that was able to place effective fires on the buildings northwest of the apartment complex as well as the western buildings of the complex. With the enemy inside the checkpoint, they were unable to get the trucks in a position where they could place effective fires upon the entire complex or the enemy positions southeast of the checkpoint. Peterson, Key, Kincaid, and Bushell dismounted and assaulted the remaining 200 meters south along the storefront, passing the pockets of pinned-down

Iraqi Army soldiers.

There were about 30 IA soldiers black on ammo (which means totally dry, out, kaput, see ya in the next life) and pinned down between the barriers and the curb. Oblique enemy fire from the apartment complex covered store-fronts, and fire from the Gold and Grizzlies traffic circle area dominated the only avenue of approach up to the storefront. Fire was coming from both four-story build-ings on the south end of the checkpoint. The volume of fire was so high it was impossible to distinguish how many PKCs and AK-47s were firing at us.

Additionally, RPGs continued to impact around the pla-toon, coming from both the alleys to the north as well as from the traffic circle area. Key carried an AT-4 on his back as they bounded south. At one point, Kincaid was able to get one of the IA armored cars to creep forward to provide mobile cover as they bounded across a 30 meter open area. The IA in the armored car panicked halfway across and backed up rapidly, leaving the fire team ex-posed. The enemy fire increased as the dismounts neared the checkpoint concrete walls, but the attack pushed the enemy back to the east side of the checkpoint.

When Key and his men got within 50 meters north of the concrete walls, neither Peterson's gun trucks nor the dismounts could observe any IA further to the southeast. So Peterson decided to seize a two-story building west of the checkpoint in order to gain observation and fields of fire across the checkpoint. Basically, he was in a building that was a block down from the building the great Beaver Platoon had used earlier.

Using smoke to conceal the 20 meters of open area, Key, Kincaid, Bushell, and Peterson did a running stack on the building and cleared it. A running stack is when you maneuver with a group of people down a street and see a door you need to get into. Upon getting there, you line up single-file. When you enter the building, you can then flow into the first room and still maintain aggression and initiative throughout your entire movement without compromising security.

Kincaid and Bushell took up positions on the second floor and began to place precision M4 and M249 fire upon enemy positions in the checkpoint and apartment complex. Key alternated positions between the second floor and the stairs. Peterson took a position on the roof with good observation of the checkpoint area. They could see muzzle flashes coming from nearly every window in the upper two floors of the apartment complex buildings as well as the tall buildings towards the traffic circle. This was across the street from their location, the same area that fire had been coming from all day. More enemy combatants were moving around the shorter buildings to the north. Peterson could see one IA soldier crouched on the backside of a mosque; others were still pinned down in front of the building they were in.

Sounds of SAF started coming from the south further toward Grizzlies but threatening the backside of the mosque. Immediately after occupying the building, PKC, PSAF, and SAF targeted our fire team in the building, with several rounds coming through the windows of the building and impacting within inches of both Kincaid and Bushell on the second floor and also around Peterson on the roof. Heavy fire from the Gold and Grizzlies traffic circle impacted on the parapet of the roof and the southeast wall of the building, bringing all to high alert status.

Enemy fire upon the building was heavy and accurate enough that all movement was by low-crawling: putting your stomach on the ground and pulling yourself along the dirt to keep as low a profile as possible. The trucks continued to take fire from the apartment complex at the one and two-story buildings north of the platoon battle position. Peterson's men pushed the trucks another 100 meters south on Route Gold so that the dismounts in the building could talk the crew-served weapons onto enemy position in the apartment complex. Talking guns are when you have two or more weapons and whatever number of rounds one gun shoots in a single burst, the other shoots the same amount. Tracer rounds from the first weapon are used to identify which target needs to be locked on by both weapons. The enemy was firing from the back parts of the rooms and interior doorways inside the building.

Key, Kincaid, Bushell, and Peterson were able to positively identify enemy positions in at least ten windows of the apartment complex as well as another six to ten enemy fighters maneuvering on the rooftops of the shorter buildings to the north. The enemy continued to fire RPGs from the apartment complex, the traffic circle, and from alleys north of the platoon. During the attack, AWT (air weapons team) Longknife came on station to support Blue Platoon and observed about twenty enemy fighters maneuvering toward Blue Platoon from the Gold and Grizzlies traffic circle. At this time, PSAF and SAF from the apartment complex increased. Concentrated 7.62 mm, .50 cal., and M203 fire did not have enough effect to suppress the enemy position in the western end of the apartment building. This prompted Key to move to the exposed rooftop in order to fire the AT-4 at the enemy position in the apartment complex.

Despite the heavy fire directed against the building, Key fired the AT-4 and destroyed the enemy position. He ran out into the middle of the open and took a courageous shot. He had to breathe slowly so that he could aim correctly and get a good shot. While he was doing this, rounds from AK fire were ricocheting by his feet and head. It would seem that Key didn't care what was being fired at him, because if he could get this one rocket out and have it impact at least within a meter of some of the insurgents, then he knew that would send a signal to the bad guys that the good guys were ticked. His AT-4 encouraged a BMP-1 used by the IA to back out of the concrete walls and engage the apartments with the vehicle's main gun. The BMP-1 would have been helpful in the fighting all along, but the Iraqis were lacking inspiration. Key's actions gave the Iraqis the inspiration that was needed. The enemy fire coming from the apartment complex immediately diminished to sporadic, but enemy fire from the traffic circle continued to be heavy. A couple minutes later, the AWT engaged the enemy at the traffic circle with two Hellfire missiles with a confirmed 11 enemy KIA.

Fire from the traffic circle diminished. Red Platoon, led by Captain Allison, linked up with Blue Platoon during the engagement. Sporadic PSAF continued to engage Peterson, Key, Kincaid, and Bushell from somewhere north of the checkpoint. Key, Kincaid, and Bushell continued to hold the building, while Peterson moved down to the street to link up Allison and Colonel Allah of the IA. Colonel Allah reported to Peterson that he had four of five BMP-1s disabled, 2 KIA, and 7 W.IA There was undoubtedly a much higher casualty count, but this is what was reported. The IA went black on ammo, and Blue Platoon was red on ammo (getting close to being dry, out, kaput, and see you in the next life). The counterattack and defense by Blue Platoon allowed the IA to cross-level ammo and regroup.

Blue Platoon used a lull in battle to cross-level water and ammo. Breaks like this are few and far between when engaging heavy enemy forces in urban combat. Weatherly pushed the trucks up to Route Gold until they were directly in front of the building so that Peterson's men could get more water for the dismounts in the building. The platoon came under RPG and SAF again.

Additionally, PSAF continued to target the dismounts in the building. Soon enemy mortars, estimated to be 81 mm, began to impact throughout the checkpoint, destroying some of the concrete barriers and one detonating about 20 meters from the vehicles on the objective. You can always tell the difference between an 81 mm mortar and a 60 mm mortar. 81s whistle when they are coming in from above because they are so much bigger. The 60s don't. At this time both Red and Blue Platoons began to break contact in order to move to support of the SOI checkpoint.

Peterson, Key, Kincaid, and Bushell vacated the building and moved back to the trucks across the open area under the concealment of smoke. As the platoon mounted up to head back to Ford, RPG and SAF erupted from the apartment complex and continued until the platoon was out of range. The platoon did not come into further contact for the rest of the patrol. Blue Platoon, consisting of four Humvees and 15 soldiers, counterattacked and then held against a skilled and determined enemy that numbered around 70 to 100 individuals. Due to the other fights in sector that day, it was 30 minutes before getting AWT support and 60 minutes before Red Platoon was able to reinforce.

The upshot of this small battle was that the insurgency carried out a plan that involved attacking all the Iraqi Army checkpoints that guarded our area along with all of the local communities. The checkpoint on Gold was the last standing checkpoint prior to our area. It would seem that the insurgency wanted to meet up and establish control of our area. Their goal was met with utter failure. This was one of many times that Charlie Company would succeed against all odds against an overwhelming force in combat which was yet another sign that the Lord was truly watching over all the men who so devoutly wished to protect and defend a foreign land, our Constitution, and our way of life.

5

A RECON TEAM LEADER'S STORY
(by John Isaac Reyes with Chris Viollette)

BEFORE he uprising in Sadr City 1-2 SCR (Stryker Cavalry Regiment) recon/sniper platoon patrolled daily in Adamiyah, Baghdad, meeting hardly any resistance in that area. Recon Platoon had only hit two IEDs in that area within seven months. Most of the soldiers in this platoon, even soldiers from the battalion or squadron, were Fallujah veterans from November of 2004.

Overall, there was a great amount of combined combat experience in the unit. In Adamiyah, our recon platoon's main mission was to fix the neighborhood. We delivered paint and barriers to schools so they could draw designs and decorate their schools. We did a lot of escort missions to different Forward Operating Bases (FOBs) as well, escorting EOD, Military Police personnel, and even Air Force personnel. As all quiet and peaceful times eventually come to an end, so, too, did ours in this area.

(March 25, 2008)

This day, which is fresh in my memory, was a day when all escort missions, paint, and barrier deliveries to schools stopped. Around 0900hrs, my unit had another escort mission to FOB Liberty in the Green Zone, and my sister and I were going to meet up again. A FOB is a base that is large enough to house multiple units, instead of one single unit. Instead, we had a change of mission. Most of the checkpoints that were being manned by the Iraqi Army were overrun by JAM or Special Groups led by none other than Muqtada Al-Sadr.

Standing by in our Strykers, we waited for an intelligence update from our platoon leader, Captain Andrew Ballow. This period of waiting brought a sense of excitement and nervousness to the whole team. SFC Christian Kiechler, the platoon sergeant, ordered the team leaders to stock up on ammunition and draw out AT-4s. I remember all too well that as soon as SFC Kiechler said, "Send some guys to the ASP (ammunition supply point) to get AT-4s so we can blow these scum bags up," there were two soldiers, SGT Johann Bloch and SGT Charles Heekin, who moved out with a great sense of urgency to fulfill the order given.

One could feel the excitement and the adrenaline pump into the platoon while everyone prepped for battle. The RTOs (radio telephone operators or "radio guys") were monitoring the radios when a transmission came over the net. "We're coming in hot!" SGT Brian Rich, one of my RTOs, heard the transmission and notified the rest of us in the immediate area. Meanwhile, we waited for CPT Ballow to come back from his initial intelligence brief. SSG Day and SGT Thomsen were debating as usual (something that happened throughout the whole 15-month deployment).

SGT Thomsen was an Arkansas Razorback fanatic. Even though in my opinion they sucked, SGT Thomsen was loyal and true to his team. I'm a Dallas Cowboy fan.

Once, Thomsen said, "SSG Reyes, Felix Jones being with Dallas is probably the best thing that's happened to Dallas ever."

I replied with the smart-ass answer, "Really dude? Because of this one guy, the whole Dallas team is now better?"

Of course, Thomsen being biased replied with a simple, "Yep."

As you can see, humor plays a role on and off the battlefield.

Finally, after standing by in the Strykers, CPT Ballow made his way back to us to give us an intelligence briefing.

"Basically, the news was that B-CO 1-2 SCR is in contact

right now, as well as the Iraqi Army near JSS UR attempting to regain the checkpoints north of Sadr City. While B-CO was out in contact, they suffered a casualty."

This is when our unit had its first KIA in this battle. SSG Joseph Gamboa at 34 years of age was killed when his platoon took indirect fire. Our platoon was ordered to stack up on ammunition and get ready to stay at JSS Sadr City with C-CO 1-2 SCR, which was located right off route Pluto. It was early afternoon when we finally arrived at JSS Sadr City. The platoon didn't even have a place to rack out (sleep); so for about two to three weeks from the day we arrived, we slept under a camouflage net with cots as beds and enjoyed the beautiful Iraqi summer as air conditioning. Microwave pizza and Pop Tarts became our main source of nourishment for the duration of our stay. I want to make this clear: I will never eat a Pop Tart or microwave pizza again in my life. That stuff tastes like dirt to me now.

While B-CO and C-CO were out in contact, rockets and mortars were impacting the IZ, or Green Zone. Our snipers, Rogue 1 element, which consisted of SSG David Dickson, SGT William McGregor, and SGT Brian Senz, were out with B-CO 1st Stryker. They were receiving SAF and RPGs.

"Feels like the whole damn city is shooting at us!" McGregor yelled as his team was making contact. Simultaneously, SSG Dickson was scanning the area when he spotted an individual guiding mortar rounds to Rouge 1's position. He immediately eliminated the threat: a 400m kill shot to the insurgent's dome is what he accomplished with great skill.

Rogue 1 was in contact before we even got our first mission in Sadr City. This made our recon platoon eager to go and join the fight with our brothers. One thing fellow infantrymen hate is if a brother is already in the fight and they are not there to support him. The recon platoon finally got our first mission in Sadr City. CPT Ballow briefed us, and our mission was to go to POO (point of origin) sites and patrol or secure them before the JAM used them again. A point of origin is used to determine the location where an indirect fire weapon was used in a hostile manner.

That evening, B-CO embarked on their mission. SSG Reyes and SSG Stahley were on the air guard hatches of their Stryker with SGT Thompsen on the .50 cal. machine gun and SGT Rich as the driver. Inside were SSG Adam Day, SPC Hank and SGT Stumma. Three other vehicles were in our convoy that followed suit. The platoon weaved back and forth through routes Texas, Bama, Florida, and Delta to check out some POO sites. As we headed north on Texas, we turned right on Route Gold. This moment is when I noticed the area was deathly quiet. My only thought was: "the silence before the storm."

My intuitive nature turned out to be correct. As the platoon traveled east on Route Gold, they started to hear SAF. It wasn't being fired toward the soldiers; so CPT

Ballow came over the radio and told the men not to shoot anything unless they had PID. As soon as our men came across the intersection on Route Gold/Delta, the vehicles in our convoy were making a U-turn and heading back in the direction of SAF.

At this point, I was gripping my M203 and waiting for the opportunity to unleash its power on the insurgency. My focus was concentrated further when SFC Kiechler announced over the radio that if you have PID you are free to engage. This put the platoon on alert but not the type of alert where a man is afraid of something. This type of alert was more like the hunter, waiting for his prey to emerge.

As we made the U-turn toward the area of contact, a bright flash, smoke, and then fire filled the air along with my senses. At the same time, the rest of our platoon called up that they were taking contact as well. That's how loud the blast was: other vehicles thought they got hit. I checked myself and was good to go; so I popped back into the hatch, saw flames on the road, and noticed that our vehicle was engulfed in flames. This is when I spotted seven enemy fighters on a rooftop of a building about 200 meters north of Route Gold from our location.

Tracers and RPGs began to fly through the air, missing SSG Stahley and myself. I told SSG Stahley to check me out because I felt a burning sensation on my arms and legs. Stahley began to pat me down and notified me that I was good; so we began to fire our weapons. My first shot went past the enemy's location, leaving no visual or audio signal. I then fired my second round, which impacted the side of the building the enemy was on. Finally, my third round went off and hit right on the rooftop of the enemy's position. Of course I couldn't confirm any kills. It was dark, but I like to think I got at least one of those bastards.

SSG Day, who was seated inside the Stryker, notified SSG Stahley to drop the ramp so as to start dismounting the vehicle. When I looked down from the hatch, I saw why we had to dismount: the engine block was hit with the EFP and was lit on fire. By then the Stryker was catching on fire; so we really had to get out before we all burned to death. As soon as Stahley dropped the ramp, more SAF was directed towards us. Once everyone was dismounted, SSG Day noticed the driver hatch was open and flames were coming out of it. My first thought was that SGT Rich was driving and the EFP impacted on that side of the Stryker. I didn't want to think the worst, but as we ducked behind the Stryker, which was the only cover we had from being exposed by the enemy, SGT Rich popped out of nowhere.

"How long have you been out here?" SSG Day questioned.

"Well," Rich (being Rich) replied, "as soon as I saw the flames trying to eat me and burnt my hair a bit, I got the hell out."

All men were now accounted for. All of us were concussed, and the adrenaline was pumping fast and fluidly. The team was mentally drained, including myself, having to deal with a ruptured eardrum.

One of the funniest moments during the ambush was when I was assessing my men to make sure no one was wounded badly. I heard the following conversation between SSG Day and CPT Ballow.

"Sir! Can I have your 9mm pistol?" SSG Day asked CPT Ballow.

"Why? Where's your weapon at?"

"It was placed next to VC seat, and that's where the flames were coming out from. Forget that!" He said this while laughing.

Meanwhile, we started to figure where we could get cover, because all of our ammunition was in the burning vehicle. Everyone could not help but wonder if and when the ammo in the vehicle was going to cook off from the heat. SSG Day ordered the team to find some cover in case the rounds or ammo in the vehicle decided to pop off. I found a shack and told my RTO, SPC Hank, to clear it with me. We did and noticed a back door to the shack; so I had Hank cover that and told him to shoot anyone that wasn't a U.S. soldier.

Apparently, SSG Day had found better cover and was yelling for me to link up with him. Being deaf from my ruptured eardrum, I didn't hear a word. SSG Day came over next to me, pulled me up to his mouth and said "Dude, what the hell? Can you hear me?" Well, the only reply a deaf man could give was, "WHAT?" He noticed I couldn't hear and pulled me to his direction, where the team linked behind a wall south of Route Gold.

C-CO was contacted to send QRF to help us out on covering sectors we couldn't man and to pull security for us while we tried to recover the Stryker. At this time, we didn't know if the enemy or the Stryker was firing upon us. The ammunition in the vehicle finally started to cook off; so we ducked and sat behind the wall until it would stop. As we waited behind the wall, SSG Day asked "Hey, don't we have an AT-4 in our vehicle?" As he asked us that question, he popped his head over the wall and BOOM!

Ducking down, SSG Day answered his question.

"Oh, hell, yep, that was it!"

While all of this was happening, we got word that C-CO was en route to our location to secure and to set up perimeters around the downed vehicle. That's when Team 2 (the soldiers in our vehicle who were hit with the EFP) began loading into the other Strykers. SSG Bonse who was manning the MK 19 40mm automatic grenade launcher asked, "How the hell did you guys get out of there alive?"

Still being deaf, I responded with, "Speak louder, dude, I'm deaf!"

Apparently when my team's vehicle got hit, the rear of the Stryker lifted off the ground and slammed back down. SSG Bonse was surprised and told me he thought when he saw our ramp drop that everyone was going to come crawling out of the vehicle with no limbs. The whole platoon remained stationary and could not move until our vehicle was recovered. It was still on fire, and ammo could be heard exploding from the heat and ricocheting inside the vehicle.

While in the process of returning to the JSS, SFC Chris Violette's platoon was headed up toward Route Gold. They were almost in the gate at the JSS when an explosion emanated in the distance, followed by a bright flash in the night from where the Recon platoon was headed. Knowing exactly what had happened, SFC Viollette ordered his platoon to speed up and to get to the site of the blast.

A man like Chris knows purely from experience what happens right away when something like this goes down. There is not a textbook or training manual that the Army can give a person to develop the nature of knowing what is involved instinctively in such an incident. Rather, this comes from experience, and experience had taught Chris well.

Stopping short of Route Gold, Violette's platoon had received the radio call from the Recon platoon sergeant stating that his element made contact with the enemy and that one of their Strykers was engulfed in flames. Upon arriving at the scene, Viollette ordered his LT along with 1st squad, 2nd squad, and a gun team into a nearby banana factory. He told his men to go there because it had a great vantage point, which enhanced the view up and down Route Gold as well as across the street.

Upon making his presence known, the enemy shifted its focus momentarily on the support that had arrived. A firefight immediately ensued. The men of SFC Violette's platoon took their own initiative and acted as a single unit in the middle of this fight. As Spartans would fight organized and strategically against an overwhelming force, so too did his men. Not one backed down from hostile fire. For a moment a few were scared, but anger at the sight of the burnt down vehicle and fear of losing a brother in combat drove them to fight the enemy with a fury that the enemy could not comprehend.

An explosion erupted 25 meters from SFC Violette's Stryker. He could not tell if it was an RPG that detonated or a grenade. Either way, it was an act of hostile intent that got the attention of all involved. SSG Ladd, who was the 2nd squad leader, identified an insurgent crawling across the street on the ground with a weapon. Without hesitation, SSG Ladd raised his M4, breathed, and fired. The round from his weapon landed directly where Ladd intended, thus eliminating the insurgent's life. It was discovered that this guy was trying to fire on the soldiers from an electrical grid while trying to reduce his silhouette.

SFC Violette's vehicle was also receiving sniper fire simultaneously from the market area and couldn't locate the shooter through its thermal imaging. The sniper almost took out an air guard (a shield that can be opened from the rear of the Stryker so that troops can get an outside view and be protected at the same time). The sniper hit the 240B mount on the back of the Stryker right next to the air guard. The squad returned fire with a grenade launcher and wiped him out along with the whole electrical grid that was later mentioned on the Pentagon Channel.

1-2 SCR's Battalion Headquarters was watching the whole thing on UAV feed and estimated that SFC Violette's platoon killed between 20 and 25 insurgents. As soon as Violette's men would take out an insurgent, the insurgents would show up on scene in an SUV, speeding down the road. Once the SUV arrived at the point where the insurgent lay dead, a few men would jump out of the vehicle, throw the body in the back, and quickly replace the dead guy in his position.

I remember well when the lead vehicle reported that they had eyes on an individual sneaking up to the side of the road 900m in front of their vehicle. SGT Guthrie, who currently was manning the 50 caliber machine gun, was scanning the objective area when he saw a suspicious individual with IED material in hand. He received authorization from CPT Ballow to eliminate the threat.

"Man, all I saw was the mist and a warm wet spot on the wall," SGT Guthrie remarked. Obviously he got the kill.

By now C-CO had already set up a perimeter around our location and pulled security for us until we could recover our Stryker. Still, the Stryker was engulfed in flames, and the rounds were being cooked off. The only gunfire we could hear was either the enemy firing at us or C-CO firing at them. We continued to hold our position until the fire of the Stryker died down enough for us to be able to recover it. Because we couldn't go anywhere, we watched the vehicle burn.

C-CO was observing a lot of activity around their perimeter with suspicious personnel and were receiving SAF while returning fire. The platoon from C-CO who came to save our ass was run by SFC Chris Violette. He and his men were the ones being pinned down and taking out hostile threats trying to get into the perimeter to disrupt our Stryker recovery.

If I remember well, in one of the C-CO Strykers, SSG Ladd and one of the squad leaders observed a man crawling about 50 meters in front of his Stryker.

"What the hell dude, are you serious? This guy can't even see us!" Ladd said with a little laugh.

Confused, Ladd continued to observe the individual. When Ladd finally got to see what this guy was doing, he saw that the man was laying wire and digging up some gravel to emplace an IED. That's when Ladd opened up with his .50 cal. and obviously sent the insurgent straight to Allah.

About 8 hours had passed since the initial blast that started this whole hectic night. When the flames of the Stryker had died down, a recovery vehicle, known as an 88M, was dispatched to aid us. The 88M is a tracked vehicle with a collapsible crane. This vehicle has the ability to mount a weapon system on it, but in most cases the focus is on the crane itself. The 88M came to tow our burnt-down Stryker back to JSS Sadr City.

As soon as we got back to the JSS, I had my ears checked out and got some extra hearing protection. Our team thought we were going to get at least a good night's sleep. Well, we were wrong.

It wasn't one hour after we returned that our unit wanted us back out in sector to secure the known POO sites. When the platoon started to head back out in sector, I was ordered to stay and seek further medical attention for my ears.

(March 26, 2008)

By this day our unit, 1-2SCR, had already lost two brave soldiers back-to-back, SSG Joseph Gamboa and CPL Steven Candelo. Both gave the ultimate sacrifice. All you can do is mourn for a bit, get your head back in the game, and continue to take care of business.

Our recon platoon was once again ordered to secure POO sites being used by the JAM. Meanwhile, I was back in the rear still recovering from my injuries. The platoon was ordered to stay out in sector, and if they made enemy contact, they were to stay in contact with the enemy. The Stryker vehicles were on the intersection of Routes Cat and Tennessee. That place looked like a ghost town. Everything was silent and kept us on our feet. Gunshots were heard all around, accompanied by explosions from other units in the area fighting.

BOOM! SSG Jean's vehicle had been hit with an RPG round. Luckily, the round didn't explode, just a bunch of sparks and debris. No one was injured. Moments after that, CPT Ballow's vehicle was hit with grenades. SPC Yeager, Team 1 RTO manning the m249 SAW (squad automatic weapon), started to scan his sector for any suspicious personnel and to find the men who threw the grenade.

While doing so, Longbow, the call sign for the air weapons team that consisted of Apaches, contacted us that they had eyes on the individuals who threw grenades at CPT Ballow's vehicle. Our platoon got the call over the radio of Longbow saying, "We got eyes on. Keep your heads down, cause we're coming in danger close and hot."

Two hellfire missiles and a 30mm machine gun were fired at the enemy. Seconds later, Longbow gave us the BDA (battle damage assessment). "Be advised; we stirred up a hornet's nest here. The locals are coming out of their mud huts and picking up the body parts from the enemy and loading them up on meat wagons, hauled by donkeys." That radio traffic basically told us the enemy was eliminated.

(March 27, 2008)

This brought us to our third day into this battle for Sadr

City with the unit's third KIA. Another brave soldier gave his all, CPL Joshua Molina. This type of pattern, given to us by death himself, could only make us wonder who would be the next to go. By this day, I was back with the recon platoon after getting my ear rocked by the massive EFP.

I only suffered a ruptured eardrum with torn layers into the eardrum, whatever that means. Our recon platoon was out again, holding and securing known POO sites. We didn't receive much contact on this day, just the usual pop shots and sporadic fire. However, our sniper element, Rogue, was out with B-CO's sniper teams, securing a building that had been blown up to be used for a hide site north of JSS UR, located north of Sadr City.

Rogue's mission was to observe and eliminate threats that have been firing mortars, RPGs, and SAF into the JSS. The first 3 hours into the hide site was calm and quiet. One of the snipers from B-CO, SGT Walters, and our sniper, SGT McGregor, took off to the third floor to make a loop hole to see the west side of the wall. SGT McGregor was holding a piece of rebar, and Walters was nailing it with a rock. Minutes later, the snipers experienced the power of an 81mm landing near their hide site.

The first round landed 100m away, and the second round landed 50m away. While SGT McGregor and SGT Walters scrambled to get cover downstairs, both were knocked down by the blast. As they quickly got back up, McGregor located the enemy spotter looking at our snipers and starting to open up with an AK-47. SSG Dickson, the Rogue 1 team leader, spotted the enemy and took him out with his sniper rifle, killing the insurgent from 300 meters away. That night, our snipers got word that they were to hold and secure that hide site for the next 2 weeks, eliminating all threats.

The next morning on March 28, 2008, Rogue 1 element was awakened to an RPG impacting the building where it was held up. Our sniper team reacted and started to scan for the enemy. They remained on high alert for two hours. During this time, SGT McGregor spotted an individual walking on a rooftop 836 meters southwest of his position with an AK-47. SSG Dickson gave McGregor the wind call and lead. McGregor fired his M24 sniper rifle. As he fired, he continued to observe. Breathing in deeply and watching his cross hairs, he closed his eyes and breathed in again. His target was still directly in his cross hairs. With his finger on the trigger he pulled it back slowly and fired the round. The bullet traveled the intended path of the marksman, his aim straight and true. Upon impact, McGregor laughingly said to Dickson "Dude that wind call you gave me was on the spot. A mist of blood popped out his head and flew to that direction." McGregor had shot the insurgent on the back of his head.

That same morning, McGregor spotted another guy with an AK-47 326m away and took him out. This morning was busy for Rogue 1. Within an hour SGT Senz saw another insurgent about 400m away also on a roof and with an AK-47. He took his shot using McGregor's M24 sniper rifle and eliminated the threat.

Throughout the remainder of the day, Rogue 1 along with B-CO snipers took heavy machine gun fire from a building located 200 meters away from the hide site. Rogue 1 began to return fire to suppress the enemy so that McGregor could take more shots with his M203 and send 40mm HEDP into that building.

He fired 6 rounds into the building, hitting every window on that side of the building. After those rounds connected with the building, the machine gun fire stopped. This same day, Alpha Company came to assist on this battle: 3rd Platoon from A-CO led by SFC Kuban. 3rd Platoon was tasked out to go overwatch an intersection on Route Cat/Tennessee. An explosion erupted in the distance. 3rd Platoon from B-CO was hit. That platoon had a downed vehicle, and Alpha Company was then ordered to go assist the Stryker with the recovery of the downed vehicle. It took no more than 20 minutes to recover the Stryker from Bravo Co. While the platoons were recovering this vehicle, the militia started engaging with pop shots every other minute. None of the rounds they fired hit any of the soldiers. 3rd Platoon A-CO hadn't had any contact since the recovery of the Stryker. While the silence consumed the area, the militia snuck up on 3rd Platoon to emplace IEDs in the area. Once the platoon began to exfiltrate, they headed back to their assigned area of over-watching an intersection.

Within 50 meters en route back to their original mission, a Stryker was hit hard with a huge explosion from an EFP. The vehicle directly behind caught the explosion on camera. One could literally see the Stryker lift off the ground as soon as it got hit. Within seconds after the explosion, the platoon began to take heavy SAF from all directions. SSG Reyna spotted muzzle flashes from about every rooftop, window, and alleyway.

The vehicle that was damaged from the EFP wasn't responding to any traffic over the radio. With the Stryker's communications down, SSG Reyna began to get in contact with a handheld radio. Communication was established, and SSG Barber responded that there were no casualties. The vehicle suffered damage to all wheels, and the engine was completely destroyed. 3rd Platoon A-CO was trying to suppress the enemy to be able to recover the downed Stryker. The platoon was quickly running out of ammo, because they were trying to kill or suppress the enemy with everything they had.

As the Strykers began to maneuver into position to begin hooking and towing the damaged Stryker, it seemed that the militia knew where to concentrate their fire, which was right on the recovery team. A platoon sergeant isn't supposed to assist on recovery. However, SFC Kuban, Haliburton, and Kellet were hooking up the Stryker to get it towed away. While doing so, all three of the soldiers were taking heavy SAF. These were not your average pop shots or rounds over your head. These rounds were hitting the Strykers and the ground near the recovery team.

The vehicle was finally hooked up and ready to be towed back to JSS Sadr City. SSG Reyna's vehicle took the lead on the way back when he spotted and then felt the impact of an explosion on a house. SSG Reyna radioed to the air weapons team to calm down on their hellfire missiles. He then notified the air team that 3rd Platoon was capable of fighting their way back to the JSS without help. Within seconds after that radio traffic, SFC Kuban's Stryker was hit with an explosion from an EFP. Not three to five seconds later, SSG Reyna in the lead Stryker took a hit with an HME ball bearing IED. All tires on the right side of his Stryker were blown out. SSG Reyna began to think to himself, "We're all going to die. Let's fight." He then spotted Charlie Co. 1-68AR, lighting up the buildings from which they had been taking contact. "Man, tankers annoy me, but not today!" Reyna said laughing.

3rd Platoon A-CO suffered only three damaged Strykers but no casualties. They killed numerous militia members and had to reload and gather more ammunition. The whole platoon was black on ammo within 30-45 minutes from all this.

(March 29 - April 18, 2008)

By now, the whole city was in contact. Units from 2nd BDE 25th IN DIV, 10th Mountain DIV, 4th ID, and

Special Operations were in the area and had their own sectors along with plenty of insurgents with which they had to deal. We had plenty of back-up and manpower: Abrams tanks, Bradleys, Strykers, MRAPs, air weapons teams, etc. No one would want to mess with us, right? Wrong!

Every unit in the area was receiving SAF, RPGs, and IDF. Around this time, our recon platoon finally got a mission that had to do with reconnaissance. We were ordered to hold down the intersection of Routes Delta/Florida. Teams 1, 2, and 3 would all dismount the Strykers and observe from a six-story apartment housing building while the Strykers locked down the traffic circle. For a good two weeks, we held that position and observed the intersection for any kind of enemy threats. No one in the platoon complained about it, because in those apartments a family would always feed us hot chow and chai (tea).

After a whole month of eating Pop Tarts and microwave pizza, we finally got some hot chow from the civilians. We thanked them every day by giving their children stuffed animals and their families baked bread. They knew why we were there and didn't mind us using their rooftops as an observation point.

The days in Sadr City began to look worse than any Hollywood war movie. This place smelled and looked ten times as bad. At one point, Team 3 was on an observation watch while Team 1 pulled security on the stairs.

My team was resting. SGT Valdovinos, Team 3 assistant team leader, started to receive PSAF (precision small arms fire).

When this happened, I had my squad designated marksman (the group's sharpshooter) assist Team 3. While SGT Bloch was scanning the area, SGT Valdovinos did the unthinkable. (It was pretty hilarious if you ask me.) He began to dance around and kept exposing his head so that maybe the enemy would shoot again and Bloch could hopefully spot him. We never found the enemy, but Valdovinos did give us all a good laugh. I remember him saying, "He's shooting at me, and I'm not bullshitting, and he's not going to hit me." We all laughed.

On April 7, 2008, our unit suffered two more losses. Bravo Company 1-2 SCR lost two more men. CPL Jason Kazarick and SGT Michael Lilly were both killed at the same time by an RPG. Our unit, 1-2 SCR had lost five men at this point during the battle for Sadr City. Early in our deployment, we lost our first soldier, SGT Randell Olguin, who was KIA in Baghdad on September 30, 2007. He was our first KIA within 1-2SCR.

After two weeks of over-watching the intersections of Route Delta/Florida, we were ordered to move up to Route Gold to provide security and assistance to the units emplacing barriers along the route. That would include three miles of road running from west to east along Route Gold. Our recon platoon, which at this time consisted of only fifteen men, was severely undermanned.

The first time we started this mission was when we had Abrams tanks in front of us that started to fire at will upon enemy targets. My Stryker was targeted again with an RPG. This time it impacted on the opposite side of the barriers that were already emplaced. While I was on the hatch of our vehicle, all I could see were muzzle flashes from weapons in all directions. I knew the enemy was north of Gold, and friendly units were south of Gold.

Once we started to set up a perimeter, it consisted of our Strykers along with two main battle tanks and one Bradley fighting vehicle, from the 4th ID's Charlie CO 1-68AR around the barriers to overwatch while the barriers were being emplaced. This is where a set rotation was implemented. One team was to pull security. The other team on the ground would assist on placing barriers, and the third would rest in the Strykers.

April 18 is when my team was the first to be on the ground and assist in placing barriers on Route Gold. We had no air support, because the air status was "RED" meaning that rotary or air support cannot fly due to weather or low visibility. It was a dust storm. SPC Hanks was pulling security along with me, and SGT Rich was hooking up the barriers and unhooking them from the cranes. SSG Stahley was on the radio with the crane operator to direct him to shift barriers. We had placed at least six barriers in thirty minutes; so we were doing great while taking SAF at the same time.

Within an hour of the mission that day, SPC Hank and

SGT Rich were hooking a barrier up from the flat bed onto the crane when we heard a loud pop. We thought it was friendly fire, but then I noticed my guys were taking PSAF. The weapon system the insurgents were using to shoot at us was a large caliber weapon. SGT Rich jumped off the flatbed and took cover while SPC Hank bravely stayed on top and continued to hook up the barrier.

We received word that 1-68 made contact earlier with the same kind of weapon, which penetrated armor on vehicles. SPC Hank finally took cover, and I said, "Dude, are you crazy?"

"What? I was almost done hooking it up," Hank said.

That's when SGT Rich jumped in and said, "Yeah good for you, dude, but I choose life."

For the next two weeks, while assisting and pulling security for the barriers to be placed along Route Gold, every team from the recon platoon received SAF, RPGs, and machine gun fire. The Abram tanks were calling up RPG teams and enemy positions to us while eliminating the threat with their main guns and suppressing the enemy with their machine guns.

While the recon platoon continued to assist on the barriers, our Rogue 1 elements headed back to the JSS Sadr City for some much needed rest and maybe to get a Pop Tart or two. Instead of rest, Rogue 1 came down on mission to support the PSYOP unit. Rogue 1 sniper team volunteered SGT McGregor to support PSYOP on manning a 240B machine gun. Their route, like everyone else's, was to head out onto Route Gold.

As the convoy headed out, they received an RPG that nearly impacted the MRAP McGregor was in. As McGregor turned his M240B towards the direction from which the round came, he saw an individual holding an AK-47 run into the house and close the door. McGregor quickly transitioned from the 240 gun to his M203 grenade launcher and fired one 40mm HEDP, impacting the door into which the insurgent ran.

Following the blast, he fired about 150 rounds of 7.62mm from M240B into the front door. The tanks and Bradley vehicles gave the enemy hell on that incident as well. After receiving RPG fire, the convoy finally reached the barriers on Route Gold to pull security. Then SSG Farina's squad from the mighty Beaver Platoon was on the ground, starting to receive PSAF from a huge weapon system that fired .50 caliber rounds. One round that was fired by the enemy ricocheted off a wall and hit a soldier's body armor, destroying it.

Luckily the soldier wasn't seriously wounded. McGregor got the direction and location of the enemy and began to suppress the insurgent, who was located in a little hut on top of a building. McGregor then transitioned back to his M203 grenade launcher and fired five HEDP rounds into that location as well. An air weapons team launched two hellfire missiles immediately after the M203 rounds were fired. Once the friendly forces finished firing, McGregor described the building in which the enemy was hiding as "Swiss cheese" because there were craters all over the building. Once again, while the snipers were taking care of business north on Sadr City, the recon platoon was still on security, overwatching and emplacing barriers along Route Gold. It was April 18th, 2008, the day my RTO SGT Rich was getting ready to go home for some well-deserved leave. Team 2 was out and about, placing barriers and pulling security. We didn't observe any threats for the whole hour we were out.

One of the funniest moments during these times had to do with SGT Rich. We had water bottles everywhere inside the Stryker. Some had water, and some didn't. Before we got out to pull security and assist with the barriers, SGT Rich urinated in one of the bottles. As we loaded up into the vehicles, SGT Rich, who was feeling thirsty, grabbed the nearest water bottle and started to drink. He spit the fluid out like a volcano went off in his mouth and yelled "S**T! Was that my own piss?" The whole vehicle was laughing, and I couldn't help commenting on the situation: "At least you go on leave tomorrow!" Even though it sucked for Rich, this was a morale booster for the team. Every once in a while, soldiers need humor during war, especially during stressful situations like the ones we experienced in Sadr City.

Late April was chaotic. After fifteen hours placing barriers on Route Gold, we finally got to go back to JSS Sadr to get some rest. My recon team and the rest of the section was napping when I had to utilize the port-a-john outside. It was around noon when I was using it and hearing weird noises. I thought to myself, "What the hell are the engineers doing now?"

I thought they were reinforcing the rooftop of the building. Then out of nowhere, two loud explosions erupted right outside my port-a-john. The door flew open, and I saw rays of light coming in through the holes the shrapnel made. I ran out of the john and ran through a hole in the concrete wall. I then ran behind an MRAP, felt two more explosions, ran into a crater, felt another two explosions, and finally made it back to link up with my recon platoon. I suffered minor shrapnel burns to the back of my neck. It stung a bit, but Doc patched me up. When I linked up with my team, everyone was under their beds. SSG Day opened his mouth first saying, "Okay, now those who never experienced this, right after this you will have what is called shell shock."

Luckily, no one was seriously wounded through this attack. These shells are known to be IRAMs (Improvised Rocket Assisted Mortars) or flying IEDs. They did not detonate on impact; each round had a time delayed fuse of ten to twenty seconds.

After this attack, early May was when everything began to settle down. We started to patrol around JSS Sadr City and overwatch routes along Delta/Florida. I wouldn't take any other man to fight next to me or bleed and sweat with me. The guys of recon platoon flexed through every mission and order thrown our way. We were different races: Black, White, Hispanic, Polish, and German. We fought and bled next to each other.

After Sadr City, our unit, 1-2 SCR, was ordered to move up north in the city of Mosul to patrol and secure the west side of the city. Hardly any fighting occurred over the last months of our deployment. C-CO killed five insurgents in the western desert area west of Mosul. The following are the teams of the Recon/Sniper Platoon 1-2 SCR:

HQ Section PSG

SFC Kiechler PL
CPT Ballow
SPC Yeager
SPC (Doc) Decker
PFC Andrade

Team 1

SSG Miller
SSG Stahley
SGT Guthrie
SGT Heekin
SGT Teal
SGT Vonbeitler

TEAM 2

SSG Day
SSG Reyes
SGT Thomsen
SGT Bloch
SGT Stumma
SGT Rich
SPC Hank

TEAM 3

SSG Jean
SGT Valdovinos
SGT Blaszczyk
SGT Wilson
SGT Burke
SPC Trovato
SPC Smith

Snipers

SFC Clanin
SSG Dickson
SSG Sivley
SGT Pence
SGT McGregor
SGT Senz
SPC Johnson

RIP to those we lost in 1-2 SCR during this battle:

SGT Olguin KIA September 30, 2007
SSG Gamboa KIA March 25, 2008
CPL Candelo KIA March 26, 2008
CPL Molina KIA March 27, 2008
SGT Kazarick KIA April 7, 2008
SGT Lilly KIA April 7, 2008
CPL Mixon KIA June 21, 2008

6

BATTLE FOR SADR CITY
(Early April 2008)

FIVE months into deployment, Charlie Company started making minimal contact around the Sadr City area. Within a month of our first shots fired, we were given a mission to link up with 1-2 SCR and continue to barrier off the southern one-third portion of the city in order to gain control of the insurgency. 1-2 had already been in theater for a year, and their unit was very seasoned in combat. By conducting this mission with them, it was understood that the need was to separate the town of Jamilla from Sadr City. The citizens, however, saw it as a wall that would divide their entire city, not simply one district from another.

All was calm in the beginning, but then after a few days of

attacks the violence increased, and the engineer unit that occupied our new location was on a mission that needed additional support. On orders to assume control of the mission, our unit was told that we were not only going to do a job we never trained for, but we would be providing our own security as well. I was told this was reminiscent of the old biblical story of Nehemiah, in which the Jews returning from captivity built a wall while holding a tool in one hand and a weapon in the other.

One of the first missions that involved the barriers was at the Delta-Gold intersection. The mission started at dusk with my squad moving barriers in the middle of the street. Shortly into the night, a sniper was spotted in a building about 200 meters from our position in a second-story window. The insurgent was not firing from the window but from the inside of the room. He had a towel wrapped around his muzzle to decrease the amount of flash that came from his weapon when he fired it.

SGT Schafer, who could be relied on for virtually any task, spotted the sniper after he fired and a noticeable signature emitted from his barrel. He told me where the guy was. Upon looking at everything that stood between our location and the sniper, the shot presented a great impossibility. No matter what the odds were, they would never trump my trust in Schafer's ability. Upon giving him clearance to take out the target, he closed in to take the shot while I remained at his side. Actually, some men in the platoon would later go on to say that it was nothing more than a lucky shot, but they were not on the ground to witness what I am about to describe.

We had vehicles in our way, power lines, and rubble from other buildings. The smallest obstacle would have thrown the round off, sending it astray. Schafer took close aim, and with one shot fired the grenade into the room with the insurgent. The round impacted to the rear of the room, exploding as it reached its target. It appeared that all time stopped until the grenade round hit its mark. The insurgent's body was thrown to the window and doubled over the opening, leaving his top half exposed.

"Schafer! How in the hell did you make that shot?" I asked with a bit of shock. "That was dead on!"

"You know how you always claim to be so good-looking? Well, I'm definitely better-looking when I fire this bad boy," Schafer replied with a smirk.

"Whatever, little boy, just keep scanning the area for the bad guys who don't shower. Oh, and there is no way with or without the help of a grenade launcher that you will ever be better-looking than me. Just can't happen, brother," I said with a pat on his back.

The building caught on fire, starting from the inside of the insurgent's hide site. Not a shot was reported from the building the rest of the night, nor for the next few days. Schafer's outstanding marksmanship kept improving through the days of heavy combat ahead, which is something all on the ground would come to rely on and respect.

On the days I was not out in sector with my squad, Lewis and his men were. He had a squad whose tactics reflected a more traditional military-style discipline, whereas my soldiers resembled a rogue band of misguided children. When Lewis and his men took fire, they stood their ground firmly and fired in a precise manner. When my men took fire, we unleashed all hell on the area until the fighting had stopped.

This is how it was every other day as we rotated coming out to the city to work. This schedule of alternating defense confused the enemy and hindered their ability to anticipate our defensive strategy. They didn't know who they were fighting, because our tactics would change every other day. This strategy also demoralized the enemy, making our victory in the War on Terrorism much more effective.

For us, however it was simple. Lewis was strict, firing only when he had to fire, mostly because he was a timid leader and had to rely more on his team leaders to get the job done. He had a complex that his father embedded in his head, telling him that he always had to be better than everyone. He was the type of leader that believed in making his soldiers respect him by berating them. The loyalty in his squad was almost non-existent. I on the other hand thought that everything needed to die, preventing as many deaths of Americans as possible. Think of it like a kill-em'-all-let-God-sort-em'-out attitude.

My philosophy was simple: if you shoot at me or my

men, not only will you die, but you will be an example to those around you. Acting on this philosophy dealt a most detrimental psychological blow to the enemy. The attacks increased over the days we built the wall around Sadr City.

As we put down more barriers, the insurgents found more places from which to attack us. After all, we were in a semi-stationary location that provided little to no cover. Sometimes we would take fire from all angles, bringing the harvest of death's appearance, and sometimes it became uncannily quiet. From the first day in sector until the last, we received almost constant enemy fire or harassment in some form. The insurgency's ultimate goal was to force the U.S. Army into retreat. We did exactly the opposite.

Continuing to lay barriers day after day, the legacy of everyone who was fighting had grown and become renowned throughout the region for defying the odds against all hope. 1-2 SCR and like units already had their hands full with epic battles taking place daily. 4th ID likewise was engaged in intense combat and set up a rotation pattern with units in the area. Soon, though, 1-6 IN would enter the scene and see the battle through to the end. With a new battalion-sized unit coming to the fight every few months, the pressure on the insurgency kept strong. It was said at one point that every man who was on the ground would receive a medal for valor (after this battle, all of the men who served did). Once word of

awards being given out got around our battalion, everyone and his brother were jumping at the gun to see some
action. Fortunately, Lewis and I maintained the integrity
of our squads and did not let people come along for a
supposed glory ride.

AEROS INTERSECTION
(April 18, 2008)

The main part of the battle consisted of twelve-hour
days on Route Gold as we pushed north, emplacing barriers on the median of the road. This was tedious work,
and the only support for the six-man ground crew was
two main battle tanks, one Bradley fighting vehicle, and
an MRAP. The tanks kept one vehicle ahead of us for
security and the other close by. The Bradley was to our
immediate front along with the command vehicle (an
MRAP.) The MRAP allowed us to have cold water and
a place where we could stock a small resupply of ammo
for the long days ahead. Vehicles moved barriers by the
truckload approximately 100 meters of our position and
then dropped them while we waited for a forklift with
another load.

Everything south of our location of the ground was considered safe. For this reason, the barriers were placed far
away from our location and required a forklift to bring
them to the site. This procedure ensured that additional

men were not required on site. A crane was placed right next to the last barrier to pick another one up, set it down, and continue. This is how we built the wall.

Two of the six men guided each barrier to the ground while the crane lowered it. The other four men positioned themselves on security. The most dreaded job of all was that of the two men who had to place the barriers in line with the others. They had to set their weapons down and rely totally upon the men next to them to provide all security. This one single factor helped the men to grow in faith and trust in each other. We ended up exactly where the Lord needed us, because this would be the site of the most fighting the country had seen in a very long time. Men who knew how to fight were the appropriate choice of men to get the job done. So we went.

Each intersection along Route Gold was given a name in the following order: Aeros was the first intersection, followed by Bravo, Charlie, Delta, and so on. Our goal was to reach Route Grizzlies, a distance of 5 miles from Aeros. Each barrier was about 2 meters wide. When a barrier was placed on the ground by a forklift, a crane operator maneuvered hooks over the top of the barrier, and one or two soldiers placed the hooks into the barrier's rebar loops. The crane operator then lifted the barrier 20 feet off the ground and aligned it with the existing wall. Soldiers on the ground then guided the barrier into position and locked it into place.

If done quickly, the whole operation to place one barrier took five minutes. However, if we received fire while placing a barrier, the process could take fifteen minutes to an hour. Our platoon picked up the mission halfway between Aeros and Bravo intersections, and thus began the long workdays ahead.

On the first day of daytime operations, I took Schafer's team in the morning. We were told to backtrack down to a place where the wall had been built earlier because the insurgency had destroyed a few of the barriers, allowing people to cross the street from Sadr City to the friendly side of Jamilla. There was about a 15-foot gap, and it was going to be a tricky project for a few reasons. Backtracking gave the insurgency time to plan a coordinated attack. In addition, the concrete barriers were not of uniform size, costing us more time to measure for a proper fit. Third, we had to check any gaps in the wall for IEDs that the insurgents placed while the wall was unsupervised. The only good thing about coming back to a previous location was a small Iraqi Army checkpoint manned with 12 men on the corner of the road where we worked. It was minimal support but more than what we had in the past. No sooner did we begin emplacing barriers than harassing fire from Sadr City would ensue. An RPG impacted south of our position about 100 meters. The concussion was enough to shake up the men around us. This was an early warning to all of us working against the insurgents that we would have to remain on full guard at all times. We began to work the barriers through the rubble that was on the ground, all the while having one of the Abrams battle tanks on the other side of the wall directly across from us to provide what support it could.

One time when a barrier was being placed, a call came over the radio that the Abrams spotted a shooter in a nearby window and asked if there were any men on the ladder on the barrier so the tank could engage. I got only part of the message over my radio. I thought I was being asked if men were on the ground working. Actually, I was being asked if men were cleared of the barrier. One of my men happened to be on the ladder trying to unhook the chain from the crane that lifted the barrier and set it in place.

When I responded, "Yes," the Abrams crew thought the "Yes" meant that we were clear. So they opened fire. The guy on the ladder was no more than ten feet from the main gun of that tank, because it was on the other side of the wall. The rest of us were on the ground either pulling security or taking to other duties while the tank fired its main gun. We felt an explosive force, much like the detonation of an IED or the impact of an RPG 29. The problem with RPG 29s is that they are not like the normal RPGs that shoot and fire in a sporadic path or fail to explode. They are capable of penetrating reactive armor and up to 750mm of steel.

In addition to being one of the more accurate weapon systems the insurgency had in its arsenal, this particular weapon carried a higher concentration of explosives that would deal a deathly blow to anything in its area of impact. This bad boy was known to do significant damage to our main battle tanks.

So in perspective, if you were in a vehicle when the round would impact, you stood a chance of feeling the effect of a rough hangover for the next few days. If one was on the ground without armored protection, it would feel like the end of a cage match at the UFC. The worst thing could be the ultimate sacrifice; so you better have said your prayers and sought forgiveness, because the next stop would be your final destination.

The man on the ladder quickly got to the ground and, like the rest of us, started wondering what had happened. We all thought an IED went off but were soon told otherwise. Communication with the vehicles was always of the utmost importance, and this small lesson that all had to learn was either to relay commands clearly or to understand what message was being relayed prior to responding. This blast was actually helpful in a way, because soon after that incident an RPG impacted the MRAP that was providing cover for us on the friendly side of town (Jamilla). Yes, this friendly side was called that because it was not as bad as the town on the other side of the wall (Sadr). It was helpful because the men were not so shaken from the concussion of the blast. It was as if the tank blast took the initial shock away from all on the ground and gave us a sense of preparation for a real attack, heightening the men's alert status, if you will.

The RPG was followed by precision small arms fire. So without being told, the men engaged appropriately. Schafer began launching a few of his grenade rounds in the direction of the enemy we had spotted in the building. The enemy set this little attack up but failed in their next task, which was to mortar our position. They sent three mortars in our direction, and all of them missed. Thank God for those men being bad shots. Because all the men on the ground had to work in such close proximity, we all would have perished or sustained serious injuries were it not for the Lord's protection. After the firing stopped, I noticed one of the IA soldiers trying to get our attention. I got Captain Looney and Sergeant Ben Rohan, and we walked over to see what was going on. The IA soldier informed us that the mortars struck nearby civilians and that the IA were trying to get an assessment of what was going on. We told them to continue with the assessment and that we would provide medical attention if needed, but we had to return to our position. Even though we sustained casualties on the battlefield, one thing we could never do was relax our security, no matter how quiet things got. As an EMT would say, "BSI, scene is safe." We always had to be on our guard like an EMT until we were at home safely in our beds.

As we continued to work on the wall and search the area for more enemies, all of the men from the Iraqi post were loading up in their vehicle. From a distance, it seemed that they were loading up everyone they could find, and

105

sure enough they were. I was wondering if these guys were tired of fighting and wanted to abandon their post, but the exact opposite was true. The Iraqi gun trucks headed to our position. As the lead truck in their convoy pulled up to Captain Looney and myself, a man popped his head out of the vehicle and said, "F***ing Arabs! They killed three women and five children. They were innocent, and they killed them! We are taking our men and are going to kill those that did this, because we know exactly where they live!"

The IA drove away, and I swear to you at that moment I had never felt greater respect for the Iraqi Army. These guys didn't care what we thought or asked our permission. They told us how they felt and what their plan was. In an instant they were gone, off to defend their country. Those men at that outpost were true patriots of their country. Those men developed a sense of patriotism because they had enough of the innocent bloodshed. This was another example of something the six o'clock news will never tell you.

7

HORSE
(April 20, 2008)

THE corching heat on this Friday morning at nearly 9 a.m. reached a temperature of almost 95 degrees, and there was much work to be done that day. When my squad arrived on the scene, we noticed a lot of green smoke canisters on the ground that could be used to our benefit. Each canister had a burn time of seven minutes and would produce enough smoke to provide thick cover if needed. We then began laying the barriers one by one until 11 a.m. came around and the temperature had risen to 110 degrees.

Directly to the northwest, on what was supposed to be the friendly side (once again, Jamilla), gunfire started coming from a nearby alleyway. The rounds impacted close to our location. Captain Looney, Sergeant Rohan, the rest of the men, and I proceeded to an alleyway north into the town. Heading west 25 meters off the main route, we began receiving heavy fire. POP! POP! CRACK! CRACK!

"Geiken, get to a spot by the corner wall ahead and return fire on the building!" I maneuvered my SAW gunner, Specialist Lance Geiken, to start suppression on the building and alleyway.

Captain Looney moved along with my men to a pile of old furniture that was on a sidewalk, allowing for plenty of cover and good eyes down the alleyway. After everyone was set, Geiken moved to our position while covering fire was provided. No sooner was everyone set in when our attackers started to engage us once more. A few of the enemy were spotted down the alleyway, and others were as close as a building directly to our front, not 15 meters from where we stood. Rohan jumped up from the cover of old furniture we were behind and immediately started firing on the enemy position. The men in the building were on a second-story room hiding behind two heavy wooden boards. Rohan, Geiken, and the rest of the men weren't intimidated one bit.

At first it seemed that something was reinforcing the wooden boards in the windows, because our rounds didn't seem to do much damage. Eventually, though, the gunmen were taken out, and we stood our ground for about 20 minutes, awaiting another attack. Rohan was on his guard with the commander during our confrontation. He never asked when to fire. He just looked for an opportunity to take out another enemy. At one time I swore I heard Rohan yell, "How do you like the taste of this rice, baby!"

When given the order, the men began to bound back in groups of two. The first two would lead off and take cover to provide security while two more men would pick up and move. All us of moved as one element: moving, setting, pulling security, and moving some more. Shoot, move, communicate was the essence of our attack method. We used this bounding technique all the way back to our barrier operation starting point which was about 200 meters away. We were able to emplace barriers for another hour until machine gun and small arms fire broke out across the street in Sadr City. There were three massive apartment complexes pushed back off the main road about 50 meters. It was from here that the insurgency would attack us. I ordered the men to halt operations and return fire on the enemy. The rounds were coming so close to our heads and bouncing off the ground at our feet that there was just no way to continue working in a safe manner. It was time to act quickly and send some bad guys home to Allah.

Captain Looney came to my side and suggested that we use the green smoke barrels as cover so that we could continue our work with a little better support. So the captain and I teamed up with one man each, and the two of us grabbed a green smoke canister and headed across the road. The two extra men provided security for us while we made a dash into the open. Once again, wherever the captain went, Rohan would be right by his side, providing cover and an extra set of eyes. As soon as the canisters were on the ground, we ignited them simultaneously, and a thick cloud of smoke came out of the top. We ran back quickly to our cover and continued operations.

This became repetitive throughout the day as the barriers were emplaced down the road. We ran out many more times to the other side of the road and set off more canisters. At times I found myself carrying the canister in one hand and holding my rifle in the other while shooting. A point we were trying to make to the insurgency was that we could continue our mission and not be discouraged by their constant harassment of fire.

Sergeant First Class Ullrich was on guard at one of the intersections in his Bradley and was at the end of his shift for the day. He was a little disappointed that he wasn't able to unleash the full potential of his crew and vehicle on the men who would threaten our lives. Lieutenant Nelson and his crew showed up to relieve Ullrich for the next four-hour shift. Less than ten minutes into the shift, Specialist Ash Cook, who was Nelson's gunner, noticed that three men down the street were setting up a tube of some sort, pointed in the direction of his vehicle. The fighting had been going on all day in the streets, and there were no civilians to be found for hours. The question posed was why in the world would three guys walk out into the daylight and point a large round object toward a coalition vehicle? Yeah, you guessed it. They were bad guys, and Cook was bent on sending them to the place all bad guys go after this life! Cook quickly notified Nelson about the situation and was immediately given permission to take care of the problem.

"Sir! I got three uglies out in the open, pointing some kind of object our way. Can I take a shot at them? Pretty please, sir. I just want one shot!" Cook begged.

"All right, Cook, fire a few rounds in their direction and make a good point that we don't like unwelcome guests in our area." Nelson allowed.

"On the way, sir!" Cook shouted as he fired multiple three-round bursts from his machine gun that was mounted on the Bradley. He began to engage with 7.62 rounds from his COAX machine gun, and then decided that these guys didn't deserve a fate as such. They needed to not only go quickly, but they also needed to be an example to others who were watching what happens when you mess with an angry infantry unit. He switched his gun from firing 7.62 rounds to high explosive 25mm rounds. Within a few short bursts of the Vulcan cannon, he watched as the rounds impacted at a high rate of speed into the chests and stomachs of the men who were the threat.

"HA! How do you like the taste of that peanut butter and jelly! Cookie three, insurgency zero!" Cook said in a victorious voice.

111

"Good job, Cook, I knew they were messing with the wrong gunner," Nelson said.

With the threat neutralized, Cook turned his attention toward the equipment so it could not be retrieved by the enemy and used at another time or place. Cook fired upon the rocket, and justice was delivered with an added bonus. When the high explosive rounds impacted the rocket pointed towards them, instead of blowing in place it somehow ignited and fired right back into Sadr City. This was something that Cook smiled about for a long time. He was able to neutralize a threat, thus displaying to the future enemy the awesomeness of the firepower he held at his fingertips, and hopefully sending the rocket back to its original maker in Sadr. Yes, Cook had a good day, a good day indeed.

SGT Payne's team entered the scene. He directed his team members individually into the shade. By the time he got to Hazelton, PKC fire opened up on their location. PKCs are the enemy's version of a machine gun used on ground troops and light vehicles. Bryant went up to the corner of the barrier to help suppress fire when he came up behind an engineer who was already locked in on a target.

The Abrams seemed to be engaging every few minutes or so at gunmen down the road who were attempting to get close to our location. They would be spotted in alleyways in groups of twos or threes. The Abrams would be sure to fire directly at them with either their .50 caliber machine gun or a canister round, which is like a really big shot gun. The tanks played the key to our outer security, and they were priceless eyes in unseen areas. They took a beating that day as well as every day. It was shocking to be working on the ground when an RPG would impact the side of an Abrams. It would shock us on the ground a good bit, but for the Abrams they just simply traversed the turret in the direction of the man who had fired the rocket and took care of business. At times, the tanks would adjust their positions and move right next to us on the ground. It was like your big brother having your back in a fight where you are outnumbered two hundred to one. The closer they stayed to us, the less RPG contact we took. However, this did make the enemy want to employ snipers. Correct employment of this asset could be as deadly as an RPG.

The fighting continued throughout the day and would increase just as the heat did. The enemy reinforced their positions in the apartment buildings, and this made things once again difficult like they had been at the IA checkpoint. Most of the enemy were afraid to flee to safety; so we had to become more accurate with target identification as time went on. By late afternoon, we had placed over 100 barriers along the route, all the while taking contact and doing our best to protect the innocent. The enemy did set up machine gun positions across the street in a few hidden alleyways, and they began to open fire on the farthest placed barrier to the north: the one we were working on.

I pulled the men back for cover and told them that we were going to have to pop around the corner and start suppressing the enemy. On my order, Hazelton and Payne button-hooked around the corner of the farthest barrier and begin suppressing the alley while Blake and I moved a little farther down ahead of the crane with no cover. There was, however, the MRAP that was the command vehicle. The men and I used the front of it as cover so we could suppress the same alleyway as well. Interlocking sectors of fire were established almost immediately, and the problem was taken care of after a few short minutes of firing. As Blake and I were scanning the area, an RPG impacted the opposite side of the MRAP. The explosive force rang like a bell, sending signals of shock through Blake's head and mine. The impact was no more than two meters in distance from where Blake and I were standing. This just shows you that MRAPS provide excellent cover and that God was watching us with a close eye.

The enemy was coordinating efforts against us, but that did not stop my squad from engaging oncoming targets. By sunset Schafer showed up with the rest of the men to relieve Payne's team and me. I trusted him enough with the rest of the squad; so I took Payne's team and headed back home. There really wasn't anything I didn't trust Schafer to do. After being out in the heat fighting all day, it was a welcome break to have someone else take control for the last few hours.

Though Schafer took his share of fire that night, I had nothing but comfort in his ability to bring all the men back safely. Besides, I needed him to step up and see what it was like to have control in case I would not be around. As a squad leader, I knew it was foolish to be the only one who could run the squad. In order for the men to survive and to be effective, someone must be able to step up and take control of the situation without question if their leader goes down.

Tribute

#SADRCITYBOYS

A few #SadrCityBoys who contributed to this com-memmorative edition by sharing memories, showing up to onsite events, reaching out to other Sadr City vets, and offering tributes.

Thank you.

SGT FELIX
S. PRIETO

CPL CHRISTOPHER DOURTE

SGT CHRIS LANDRY

SSG EDWARD
A. HARMES

SPC CLIFTON E. HOFFMANN

SSG DARREN
LESLIE

SGT JAMES
A. STANFORD

SGT LANCE
E. LOREY

SPC PAUL
RIDER

8

BRAVO INTERSECTION
(April 27, 2008)

CHARLIE company arrived at a road intersection that would become known as the most deadly of places: we referred to it as the Bravo Intersection. This was the day of the most brutal attack that I and many others had witnessed. The firefights started at 10 a.m. with temperatures in the high 90s along with increasing sniper fire and RPG attacks that went on for hours. The insurgents did this to distract us so that they could set up secure positions inside buildings to our immediate front. At about 1 p.m. everything erupted in small arms, RPG, and sniper fire. I remember shortly before the chaotic eruption of fire that I was checking my watch and wondering why the day was dragging on. From 10 a.m. to 1 p.m. it felt like over twelve hours.

Constantly maneuvering the men around to different

locations made for tedious work in order to suppress one area while covering another. I kept thinking that if it was my time, then God was going to take me. Later in the fight, Hazelton spotted a man holding an AK on a rooftop near a water tank. We had been taking fire from his location; so I ordered the Abrams battle tank to open fire on his location. The men in the vehicles had a hard time understanding exactly which water tank I was talking about; so I along with Blake and Hazleton engaged the area where the man was. This helped to confirm his location, and the Abrams was able to unload a main gun round on top of the building. This gave the men on the ground a bit of a morale boost. However, to the left of the location in another building that we had been firing on, the enemy took up positions and started to engage all of us who were on the ground.

Then it happened.

A man came around the corner with an RPG and shot at the crane that was placing the barriers. Blake and I were right behind the crane. The rocket impacted, sending shrapnel downward. A piece of shrapnel ricocheted off the crane and slammed into my neck. I remember thinking that someone had just put out a cigarette on the center of my neck. The scar today serves as a reminder of this incident. None of the shrapnel hit Blake, surprisingly. I had body armor on, but the blast had shot at a downward angle. At this point it was roughly 3 p.m., and we had been on a constant adrenaline rush for six hours in 100+ degree weather.

Time seemed to have stopped as the rocket impacted the huge piece of iron above my head. BOOM! Blake looked at me and told me I was bleeding from the neck. I fell backward and started shaking, unable to breathe. I held my neck. When I removed my hand, I saw blood covering my palm.

"Mark! Mark! I'm hit! I'm struggling to breathe!" I gasped over the radio to Staff Sergeant Mark Peck.

I heard in reply, "I got ya, Tony. Where are they at? We'll make them pay!" Peck said in an angry voice.

I tried to respond but was in a bit of shock and could not think clearly on what to do next. I just lay there and thought that surely this was it: I'm going home. Blake was the first to come to my aid with a bandage in hand. He asked to see the wound. Instead of complying, I was swatting his hands away from my neck. Meanwhile, Hazelton was trying to work my handheld radio, and Blake was trying to be a medic and not get shot because the real medic showed up, took one look, and ran away saying, "Bring him to the MRAP."

Bring him to the MRAP? I thought to myself. What are you trained to do? Assess the casualty and run, or assess the casualty and, well, run?

Payne and Blake took me to a medevac vehicle to get checked out. First Sergeant Gonzales was waiting in the MRAP, providing me with medical attention and checking to see how deep the shrapnel wound was. Gonzales was on the radio constantly with the TOC, coordinating actions on the ground as well as relaying my status.

I started to think about an important event that took place prior to coming to Iraq: the day my grandmother gave me her rosary. I was visiting her and my grandfather in Hammond, Indiana, just a few days before shipping out to Iraq. As I awoke at 3 a.m. to get on the plane to go back to the Springs, she took my hand and put a wooden rosary in it, saying that it would bring me protection. For some reason, I had left my rosary in my quarters the morning of this battle. That was odd, because I always had it with me in a pocket of my uniform.

Prior to departing for the day, I noticed at the gate of COP Ford that I had left my rosary in my room. I asked our platoon sergeant, Sergeant First Class Ullrich, if he could stop the convoy for one minute so I could run back in to get it. Reluctantly, he did what I asked, and now I am ever grateful he did. Ordinarily, when a convoy calls up that they are ready to go out on a mission, you do not stop for anything. On this day, Ullrich did. He stopped the convoy as a favor, and I firmly believe the Holy Mother Mary is to be thanked for saving my life.

The team then took cover in a nearby shack to devise a plan while Captain Looney grabbed four 84 mm AT-4 rockets and began to engage everything. Staff Sergeant Peck jumped onto the ground to coordinate fires more accurately, eventually pinpointing the location of the shooter from the alleyway. Peck was a Bradley commander of great skill as well as the rest of his crew. His gunner, Sergeant Jay Gold, was an expert with his weapon system, and his driver, Private First Class James Lafollette, could traverse and park the 30-some-ton vehicle on a dime. Together they would bring death to those who would harm the men who were trying to do something good for the area.

Peck had Blake pull security while Payne followed the commander on the ground to engage targets from all locations without cover and without any fear of losing their lives. This is what makes fellow infantrymen so great: you hurt one, and the rest get really, really mad. After a few minutes I noticed the fighting had picked up even more, mostly because my brothers on the battlefield were very upset. I was given the option to stay in the recovery vehicle and not go back out to the fighting. It was then that Geiken fired a long burst into a building for cover. I saw the rest of the men, and they seemed displaced. I refused medical attention and jumped back on the ground with my men.

They were all shocked when I came back out and said, "Didn't think you could get rid of me that easy, did ya? Heck no, your daddy's not going anywhere, ladies." That's exactly how I said it, and if I could tell you how I found humor in that moment, I would explain it. But I can't.

The main battle tanks opened up on target buildings, firing multiple rounds. The explosions from their guns and the Bradley fighting vehicles literally shook the whole ground. Trying to reload my weapon, I dropped a magazine or two. This was because my hearing protection had fallen out from all the sweat, and the noise from the blast was so deafening that it shook my inner core.

When Peck heard over the radio that I had been hit, he took his gloves off and unleashed everything short of God's fury on the enemy. He guided his men to fire with precision in every direction. I was impressed as one of my riflemen on the ground remained very focused throughout the point of chaos. Hazelton was able to spot two men in different locations who were shooting at us from rooftops. He guided the men in the armored vehicles to the exact location so they could be engaged effectively.

The enemy body count that day was somewhere in the low 30s. You could literally begin to smell the scent of death in the air as the day went on. The battle continued until we were approved for air support, and then death from above rained on the enemy. This seemed to give the men a renewed sense of courage and spirit. They fought harder than ever for the next hour, until we were able to call in air strikes on the immediate vicinity. The battle was over by 3:00 p.m.

I was taken back to the aid station, and our company's medic documented my wound. I remember sitting on the gurney, looking at my blood-soaked shirt. The blood was thick at the neck and came down to a "V" on my chest. When Doc appeared, he had me lay back on the table to examine me in more detail. CPT Looney came in and asked the Doc to sew me up after the shrapnel was taken out of my neck. My head was hurting, and I was in pain. But CPT Looney did one great job of stitching me up. I was given some pain medication for the night and returned to duty the next day. That night as I fell asleep, I kept hearing the cracking of gunfire, and my head would shake when I was resting in my bed. It felt like I was next to an explosion each time my head got that shaking feeling. I slept through the night and went back out the next morning, very thankful that my wounds were only minor.

(April 28, 2008)

On the next day out, Ullrich and Fox manned the Bradley that would be pulling security for the men on the ground as usual. About two hours into the shift, an explosion from an RPG hit the wall on the left side of the road, which was the opposite side of the barriers from where the men were. Captain Alan Boyes called over the radio that an RPG was launched from the Sadr City side of the road very close to the Bradley.

Fox began to scan diligently with the turret of his vehicle, and he noticed a three-story building with an open bay window that was on the left side of the building. He could see all the way into the room and noticed that a door was wide open. He then scanned the building from left to right. As he came back, he noticed the same door was closed, giving away the position of where the target was hiding. He informed Ullrich that the man who had fired the RPG had just looked out the closed door in the battle-torn building. Fox was not going to let this man get another shot at his vehicle or the men on the ground. He quickly fired his machine-gun into the room to suppress the man inside.

All the while, Ullrich was telling the main tank directly below the building to back out of the firing zone. As the tank moved out, Fox used the high explosive ammunition to take care of the remainder of the threat in the building. This is how close the insurgency would dare to come simply to get a shot at the men who were building the wall. This is one example of how quickly our men in the vehicle would react to engage and destroy the threat.

Later that day, Lewis's team had to continue laying barriers across Bravo intersection. They got on the ground and started placing barriers on the south side of Bravo and then moved to the north side of Bravo to build a barricade they could use for protection during the night. Lewis' men had to work with their boots covered to their ankles in the enormous amount of sewage from the bombing the night before. The building that was hit earlier was still on fire, and in that building was a cache of weaponry that was firing off. Moving north on Charlie, Lewis's squad took sporadic fire all day. It was right around the middle of the day when Sergeant Patrick Simpson came out with his team, and they drew closer to the Charlie/Gold intersection.

Specialist Moses and Lewis were putting barriers on the ground when a loud boom went off. A tire flew up in the air, and a piece of concrete hit Lewis in the leg. Lewis was given the word to finish up barrier operations. He then ordered Moses to get back on the ladder and finish the mission.

Moses had to ask not only a second but third time what the exact order was. What Moses said next sounded something like, "Ah, dude, this is bull****, dude this is BULL****, DUDE THIS IS BULL****."

All the while, Lewis was laughing and telling him, "Hey, you don't get paid a dollar a day for nothing now, do ya?"

Moses reluctantly went back on the barrier and finished the mission. While Lewis and his crew were on the ground, I showed up to relieve the current Bradley crew that was in support of the operations. As squad leaders, Lewis and I were required to be proficient not only on the ground but in a Bradley fighting vehicle as well. As day turned to night, I would scan the area and be trained by one of the company's better gunners, Corporal Gary Muckelvaney. We had to look down a particular alleyway and scan for the enemy so that they could not sneak up on the men who were working on the ground, as had been done before.

Our vehicle was meters forward of the men on the ground so as to get a better view of a hidden alley and act as a shield if necessary. Right next to us was an Abrams that was taking up another security position. This helped to make the intimidation factor much higher in the immediate area and ensured that there were three sets of eyes in every direction for security.

As the sun slid below the Iraqi horizon, the night was welcomed in, bringing cool relief to the men and my sweat-soaked body. In the cramped turret compartment of our Bradley, Muck, and I sat shoulder-to-shoulder scanning the area. Muck was giving me lessons on the different types of controls used at night. The green glow of the turret control panel gave our faces a twisted, ghoulish look. The dried sweat from the day was stinging my eyes as I stared into the night. The alleyway in front of us played shadow games with our minds.

Through our night optics, we noticed a cat creeping out of a hidden doorway, checking the area for food. I sat watching the cat do his thing, my night vision giving him a sickly green hue. "Aw! Hello, little kitty. What are you doing?" Before the kitty could answer, I screamed, "RPG!"

A dark figure had stepped around the corner in a fast motion with a rocket propelled grenade on his shoulder, trying to aim in our direction for a quick shot. Whether his intent was to harass or kill us did not matter, because as soon as I shouted "RPG," my hand was already releasing the fury of the Bradley's main gun. The force of the three rapid 25 mm rounds leaving the barrel shook my body. The shock wave from firing the rounds produced smoke and dust that filled the small turret. The expended gunpowder burned my lungs as I was trying to breathe.

When I could see clearly, I saw the first round hit the dirt by the man's left foot, the second went straight into his chest, and the third round hit somewhere between his waist and stomach. The violent impact flung him back, twisting him like a rag doll. The 25mm projectiles punched two baseball-sized holes through his torso. His body lay on the ground, cold and lifeless. We kept an eye on him for any signs of movement. There were none.

When the smoke cleared, I used a mild sense of humor to deal with the situation by calling over the radio to all the men in the Abrams: "Infantry one, Tankers zero!" Then I heard a few other responses of how the man had already been locked in the sights of men in the Abrams vehicle next to us. I could hear a hint of jealousy in their voices from their exchange, because this was what every man in a turret of an armored vehicle trains for: the opportunity for the perfect shot at an insurgent who would do us harm. This was not in any way the first time I had ever shot or killed a man in combat.

In truth, I do not know how many lives I was responsible for taking. This is one example of how we soldiers stop terrorism. We find the bad guys, and we kill them. There is no other way to put it.

Battles like this would continue as we laid barriers through the city. The deadliest parts were the intersections, because they provided the least amount of cover. To our benefit, we caught onto this early in the game, and we knew that every time we would come up to an intersection of two main roads in the city, we were going to face some resistance. There was a day when all seemed quiet for a change (the first day the ceasefire was in effect). The ceasefire lasted about a whopping ten hours, and then the first IED went off. We had to halt barrier operations many times that day because of the explosions.

What I am going to tell you next is the best testimony of divine intervention that I have ever experienced or can possibly describe. Our men were doing their usual work, and Schafer spotted a man coming towards our location. He shouted to the man and received no response. The man appeared to have some kind of handicap, because he walked with a sort of limp in his step. Schaefer fired a warning shot at him. When he did not stop moving, Schaefer fired another shot right next to his foot. The man then squatted on the ground and covered his head, not moving.

Bryant wanted to get the man to move out of the area as well, so he threw a smoke grenade toward him. The spark from the fuse of the grenade landed on something that ignited a nearby shack into flames, and within a minute a burst of flame erupted on the ground along with a small explosion. Captain Looney noticed there was an eight-inch copper disk on the ground, and the burst of flame turned out to be homemade explosives that were packed into an EFP. Multiple flames shot up from different areas on the ground next to our position. This is why I say it was divine intervention, because those were bombs set to detonate on the men close to them. They never exploded.

Minutes before this incident, the rest of the men on the ground and I had been standing in front of the location of the explosion. Once again, our good fortune confirmed to us that we were receiving help from above. Then as usual, the RPG games went into effect along with precision small arms fire. After returning fire and gaining a foothold on the situation, I pulled the men to a covered location and ceased barrier operations. In the immediate area, more IEDs were being discovered close to our location. We used an old shop for cover and waited for word on when the rest of the route would be clear so that we could continue working.

It would be senseless to keep the men out on the street while there were still active EFPs hidden from us, so we remained in cover. We moved out of the building periodically to see if we could commence operations, only to find ourselves in another engagement with the enemy. Instead of going back in for cover, we found some barriers that were stacked close to the MRAP and returned fire on the rooftops.

An hour or so went by before our relief showed up. When they arrived, an IED went off in the median about 100 meters ahead of our position. I distinctly remember seeing a tire fly in the air, which made me wonder if an Abrams had taken a direct hit. There was a big cloud of smoke from the explosion, and then a wall of gunfire erupted from the Sadr City side. It was the loudest and longest fusillade of small arms and machine gunfire I had ever heard in one volley.

My squad held our positions until the gunfire ceased, at which point we returned fire and then were ordered to mount up into the vehicle to return to base. The new unit had assumed command and was taking over the operation for the rest of the night. When the day was over, I later found out that in the same area less than 50 meters down the stretch of road, there had been six IEDs that were set to detonate on me and the other men on the ground. Throughout the day we walked right past all of the IEDs that were in place. Not one ever went off. During the entire time I had been in sector for roughly two months, there was rarely an IED that failed to detonate, if any at all.

After enduring what I had to go through and witnessing the odds of walking out of this place alive, I knew only one thing: the Lord was providing the security for me and the men on the ground when we could not provide it for ourselves. I began to feel more confident in combat, knowing that for some reason or another, all that I had been put through up to this point meant that I was surely not meant to perish in this country yet. I had a job to do. However, I did not know what it was. I was being kept alive and watched over by the angels the Lord had sent to protect us. Heavenly hosts kept guard over the men and protected us from the unseen forces of evil which would do liberty and justice harm.

(May 2, 2008)

Pulling up to the Delta Gold intersection, SSG Mike Briggs' Abrams battle tank stood guard on the side of Route Gold that had been receiving the most contact from enemy forces. He heard his tank commander tell him to shift the tank to the 11 o'clock position so that they would be facing north. As soon as he did this, Mike spotted an insurgent peeking out from an alley about one hundred meters away.

The battle tank's gunner, SGT Bartley, saw him but surprisingly didn't engage. It was a rare moment for the crew not to fire a main gun round at a peeker (insurgents who would try to sneak a peek at coalition forces on patrol). About ten minutes late, the insurgent stepped around a corner with an RPG, faced the tank, and fired. As this happened, the right side of the tank exploded, followed by another explosion to the front of our vehicle: a dual impact that shocked us all to our core. The crew felt the shock harder than normal, due to the fact that they did not have their hatches closed.

Both RPGs hit beside the driver's hatch; so all the concussion came in through the driver's hole and out the loader's hatch. When this happened, it temporarily knocked SSG Briggs and the loader, SPC Vazquez, out cold. Upon regaining consciousness, Mike noticed that the tank behind his was firing its main gun, the 120mm cannon. The dust and smoke that filled the inside of the tank made it extremely hard to breathe for all inside the vehicle.

One thing that guys like Mike Briggs do to keep their sanity during high intensity missions is to keep pictures of family with them. Mike would use the picture of his family to take him to his own happy place. On the morning of May 2nd, Mike had finished a wrestling session in the gym at COP Ford with SPC Vazquez, then he went to sit in the driver's seat of his tank and stare at the picture of his family.

Mike wanted to be with his family that morning; so he did the next best thing he could do. He sat next to the picture in his driver's hole, faced away from the picture and smiled (as if he were right in the picture with them), and snapped a quick photo.

This moment in time froze for a second, and after a few moments of having his guard down in combat, Mike and his crew were sent off into Sadr where the events that I described above happened throughout that day. To Mike, this is what he told me was the last picture possibility. He described this best in an e-mail to me when he was talking about what it was like for him to go through combat for the first time. Here are his words:

Back to the fear thing: the best way I have found to describe it is this: your life doesn't flash before your eyes like in the movies. However, it is every emotion at one time, and with these emotions you place images to best convey the emotions to yourself. It's a weird feeling. So for the next few days, the aid station pretty much just kept SPC Vazquez and myself medicated. When you go months seeing people explode from a 120mm round, EFPs blowing people up like Rice Krispies, and your infantry guys on the ground, depending on our superior firepower to a certain extent, these aren't daily events. This is sensory numbing. With that much adrenaline, or emotions, they weren't crazy days. Combat affects everyone differently. I personally will never forget those months. And what you are doing is amazing; it's almost like therapy without talking.

Around the same day, a gunner named SSG Ryan Healy worked with SFC Miller, a tank commander. The driver on this day was SPC Vazquez, who was usually a loader and also the same SPC Vazquez who worked with SSG Briggs. He wanted to drive on this day; so the loader was PFC Costa. One night at around 1730, SFC Miller's platoon went out on patrol to relieve another tank crew. They were pulling twelve-hour shifts, guarding the troops from C Co 1-68 and 1-2 SCR on the ground while the wall was being built. It began to get dark; so SSG Healy switched over from the day sight to the thermal sight. They were probably sitting for a couple of hours before anything happened. It was past curfew; so the crew knew that they had permission to engage if they saw anything unusual. At this point, everyone was goofing around, trying to kill boredom. All of the sudden, I saw a hot spot in the corner of my sight that I quickly scanned. The hot spot disappeared. SFC Miller asked me what I had seen. I told him I saw a hot spot and asked him if he trusted me.

"Of course, I trust you."

"Good, then can I try something?"

He instantly wanted to know what I was planning. Having no time to explain exactly what needed to be done, SSG Healy just said, "TRUST ME." With permission to test out the idea, SSG Healy proceeded. He told PFC Costa to shout the command when the main gun was armed. Scanning back to his original position, SSG Healy pretended he saw nothing, even though he noticed movement out of the corner of his eye. He slowly switched weapons from his main gun of 120mm to his COAX of 7.62 mm machine gun. All Healy could do at this point was to wait for the insurgent to pop around the corner again.

Then it happened. The insurgent jumped out from behind a generator and started firing an AK-47 at Healy's tank. Healy, laughing, traversed his turret in the direction of the insurgent and pulled the trigger, activating the machine gun. The rounds from the COAX swept across the insurgent's knees. When that happened, the insurgent tried to get back behind the generator. Still having the tank in COAX mode, Healy grabbed the Master Blaster (basically another way to fire the main gun if all else fails), turned, and shot an MPAT round at the generator. Healy had to keep both triggers depressed to make this work. By doing this, he fired the machine gun and shot the main gun at the same time. As far as I know, this had never before been attempted. Everyone I told about this also said they had never heard of this being tried as far as they knew. After Healy finished firing the rounds, the tank started blinking lights, and the machine gun stopped firing because the COAX circuit breaker had been tripped.

"What the hell did you just do, Healy?" said SFC Miller. Healy explained and told him that he wanted to see if this would work, and it did. Needless to say, the insurgent didn't make it.

9

REUNION

SERGEANT First Class Chad Urquhart was his name, and he was a squad leader of mine during the invasion of Baghdad in 2003. Chad had changed a lot since those days. Now he was more understanding. Back in the invasion, he was a fresh new squad leader in the Army, and he was very demanding of his men. The men who had died in our platoon in the invasion, whose deaths I sought to avenge, were members of Urquhart's squad. He, too, still shared the same wound that I carried from so long ago. When his unit came to COP Ford and I saw him for the first time in over three years, all the things that went wrong between us had suddenly vanished. I felt no more anger or hatred toward him as I once did.

My forgiveness echoed with his presence at my side. My anger with Chad went all the way back to when he was my squad leader during the invasion. He was in charge of the four men who lost their lives to the first suicide bomber in the invasion. I blamed Chad for this because I had no one else to blame. Through time, my hatred for him grew. Eventually, I was able to see that Baghdad was not just a place of war and hate. For me, it was a place where I could find forgiveness and give it freely.

It felt good to forgive after holding that grudge and anger in for so long. We spent the first day in a reunion of sorts, catching up on old times and talking about who went off and did what with their lives. We joked about the little things that used to set us off in the past, how things were so trivial, and how we could not fathom how one could get angry at the little idiosyncrasies of the past. No, the only thing that mattered was that for the first time in months I had some form of family from my past here with me. That can be the most comforting feeling when you have to endure this war day in and day out, not knowing if you are going to see your biological family again. Chad filled that missing link out here. He was my brother from the beginning and still remains so today.

The next day, he went out to the city with his commander and the rest of my men. My men began showing him the ropes on how to emplace the barriers properly and still set up a sound 360-degree defense of the immediate area. The day grew hot very quickly, and I could see in Chad's face what I felt to myself so many weeks ago when this had all started: nostalgia. The heat was one thing a man could depend on in the day; we knew the hours when it would become the hottest and the hours when things would cool down. Chad would quickly adapt to the environment, and we would still laugh and joke about where we were.

He remembered our time back in the same area in Sadr City and embraced those memories. I knew he was thinking hard for the first few hours, because he was a bit silent and looking all around like an eager child at an amusement park. This is what struck me about Chad. Here we were in the middle of the worst place on earth, and he would be all happy, picking out certain buildings and locations that seemed familiar. He even noticed the green, onion-looking building where, back in the invasion, we were awarded our Combat Infantry Badges. Back then, we were members of a well-respected platoon, and here we were again on the same ground where the fighting had happened before, still in respected units.

Once again within only a few hours of our presence in the city, we were receiving harassing sniper fire from a few nearby buildings. This made matters a bit more difficult today, because at this particular location the buildings where the firing was coming from seemed to be a bit close. The buildings were on the friendly side of our location, and the shots were not coming from one location. They were coming from multiple locations. The enemy had somehow learned that if they harassed us enough, our attention would be diverted from our work of building the wall, allowing them to seize the chance for a better defense on future attacks.

The enemy spent some time setting in and taking shots just close enough to barely miss us. However, it was close enough for us to have permission to engage. For the ten-plus men who were on the ground, we began firing, and the enemy's plan came into play. Once we started firing, insurgents in other locations were able to pinpoint more accurately where individual soldiers were on the ground. We began to increase our firing in multiple directions, further engaging more locations and more of the enemy.

Chad was right by my side through all of this. He even spotted some enemies who were on my blind side, trying to take a shot at my men and me. He then engaged them with such accuracy and ferocity that the enemy often didn't want to fire back. When I witnessed Chad fighting, it filled me with a sense of heroic courage to a point where I would do the same thing I did at the Bravo intersection: devise a plan and expose myself so as to gain ground for a better shot and another chance to stop terrorism.

After about a half an hour of moving from covered position to covered position in such a small area, I called up the forklift over the radio, the one that carried the barriers from the trucks that hauled them to our location. I told him to stack two barriers, one on top of another in a certain location that was out in the open. This position was roughly about 25 meters away from where we had initially been fighting and setting up defense. The forklift was perfect for this, because the vehicle had added armor that could withstand sniper fire with no problem.

As a matter of fact, this same forklift driver had proven his worth to us many times over during the entire conflict. He was a good ol' boy who was not afraid to come to our aid when we needed him. He would get out of his vehicle when asked and provide us a hand in securing whatever equipment we needed, no matter what or how much was being fired at us. He would be the same driver who would later get stuck in some wire and sit tight in his vehicle as a massive firefight would ensue.

Main gun rounds from our battle tanks would shoot dangerously close to his vehicle, and this man would never falter. At Bravo's intersection right before I took shrapnel from the RPG, this driver had his vehicle placed as cover for our men, and the vehicle miraculously withstood two direct hits from RPGs. He drove away that day with a flattened tire. But his morale was still high, and his spirit was still in the game.

While the fork driver placed the barriers as I instructed him in a manner that set up my future defensive position, I gathered all on the ground to tell them of my quick plan. (I was not sure if it was going to work, but it was a plan nonetheless.) One thing you should know about combat is that indecisiveness can kill you, while a bad decision will only wound you. This turned out to be neither, and it worked like a charm.

I had Chad and his commander lay down suppressive

fire in one location while the rest of my men covered down on other sectors. I took my team leader, Schafer, who I said before was a master with his M203 grenade launcher, moving him along with myself to the barriers that were stacked up. This location gave us direct line of sight to a sniper's location. Fire suppression for cover was quickly laid down while Schafer and I moved to our location, all the while hearing bullets fly over our heads and impacting on the ground close by. Once we got to our covered position, I aimed at the window where the sniper was and fired roughly 20 rounds. This tactic was not only that the sniper would be shocked that we were so close, but it was to give Schafer a chance to expose himself as much as he needed in order to get a clear shot off from his M203.

The shot was difficult but not unlike anything Schafer had encountered before. It was a small building on a roof, sheltered by two huge palm trees. There was only one window that was big enough for a medium-sized man to crawl through. This was a good location for a sniper, because it gave him a close-by, elevated position. It also offered cover for the small place in which he could expose himself.

As I told Schafer I was about to reload, I ducked down and slid the empty magazine behind my knee. As I closed my leg on it, I went into a kneeling position. I immediately grabbed a new magazine and jumped back up to see Schafer fire the lethal shot. It impacted directly where I told him to aim; it went exactly where he intended it to go. That was how Schafer did things.

That same night, a news crew from NBC was sent to the COP to come out and play with the boys because they had heard about what was happening down here in our area. They were introduced to the leadership of Steel Company as well as the men who would be escorting them for the evening, the Beavers. After spending a night at the COP and getting a feel for the atmosphere and living conditions that surrounded the men, the three-man news crew loaded up with Lewis's squad to head out to the wall.

On this particular day, the wall was about 200 meters shy of the Delta intersection, roughly a few building lengths further than we were the night before. I would be commanding the Bradley fighting vehicle that would carry Lewis and his men, while the news crew would be in the MRAP with Captain Boyes. The two Abrams would escort us with front and rear security, sit in position, and relieve the other vehicles of their duties when we got to our destination.

I could only guess that for the first few hours the news crew must have been wondering what the big deal was about the wall, because on our way out to man our shift the route clearance unit ahead of us encountered multiple IEDs and had to clear them before we could proceed. This would go on for about two hours just to clear roughly one mile of road. When we did finally get to our desired location at the farthest point of construction of the wall, all men got out of the vehicles, including the NBC crew and Captain Boyes.

One Abrams went ahead to the Delta intersection to stand guard, while the other took up security to the right flank on the other side of the wall where the men were operating. I had Specialist Galloway, the driver of the vehicle, pull forward about 15 meters of where the men on the ground were to provide immediate support and close security. As barriers were placed, the news crew started wandering around and almost crossed to the Sadr City side.

Two hours into the mission had not yet gone by when the first gunshots rang out from the Delta intersection, shots that were aimed toward the men on the ground. Sergeant Ziska and Nguyen immediately engaged the windows of the buildings. The other men followed suit. All the while, Lewis was guiding the rest of the men to start operations without letting the enemy see that they would be stopped by mere gunfire. The news crew started filming almost immediately and tried their best to report what was happening over the loud firing of small arms and automatic weapons.

Muck was with me in the turret, scanning actively to the immediate left of the men, looking for secondary attackers. Sure enough, they popped up on rooftops and in windows as soon as Ziska and Nguyen had finished firing at the targets down the street. When the firing started from the left, Captain Boyes and Lewis started firing with much aggression in an attempt to gain fire superiority. Lewis drew his men back and had them take up covered locations to engage in interlocking sectors of fire on the multiple buildings from which they were being attacked. I was given guidance over the radio by Lewis when firing from the left buildings started. I was able to spot two confirmed targets and a possible third. I ordered Muck to engage with 25MM HE at one building in order to knock out the shooters on the roof. After that was completed, I scanned farther to my left, which put me right on a building that was due southwest of their position on the ground. I told Muck at this point to let me engage, because I had a personal issue with the shooter in this building.

I wanted to engage this target myself, because we had taken a lot of fire from this exact building the day prior. I had felt numerous bullets that day come very close to my head and feet on the ground. I wanted to make sure the job got done once and for all. What made it more difficult for the men on the ground to attack the shooter from this angle was that there were two huge palm trees that formed an arc, covering the top floor balcony. My first instinct was to leave the ammunition selection on "High Explosive" and start doing a little landscaping. I held down the trigger, firing some ten rounds from right to left with the turret, directly into the upper level of the house. This made a clear view of the insurgent. I finished

153

the job with a few more high explosive rounds to the lower level of the house so he could not have an easy escape if he made it through all that alive.

This firefight was over for now; so Lewis had the men continue to emplace barriers along the route. When they had gotten a few more on the ground, Lewis whipped out a can of spray paint and made our mark: the mark of the platoon that will live forever in that city. He spray painted in rather large writing the words BEAVER DAM. Because our platoon was given the name of Beavers, we saw fit to let the enemy know who was out there all of those days kicking their butts.

Captain Boyes would later put the battalion's unit crest right between two barriers as they were being set in place. This was another way of telling the people that we had been here. It was also a way to leave something in place, permanently, that symbolized freedom. When the wall was eventually finished, we found out that the locals unintentionally painted the wall blue. Blue is the color of the infantry, and to us it was a way the Lord said that we had done a good job and that He was with us every day that we were out there. The locals have no idea what the color blue represents, but that still has a lot of meaning to us. To me personally it meant we were not alone on those dark days.

The shooting became more random and less focused as the hours went on, yet the shooting was enough to keep Lewis' men alert and on their feet. Nothing bad enough happened to hinder barrier operations as the city burnt in the background. As I recalled later when I would think about the long days of battle more in depth, I could not think of a day when the city was not aflame at night. Yes, every night that we went out, the city would burn. It burned not because we intended it to. It burned because men in that city threatened America, and the men in our company would eliminate that threat daily.

10

DELTA INTERSECTION

THE next few days were rather quiet until we reached our starting point of the whole operation (which would be our last). This was called the Delta Intersection. To give you an idea, on one corner there was an Iraqi Army compound, while on another was a semi-friendly neighborhood, and on the opposing side was Sadr City in all its glory.

We started our barrier operations early in the day, ensuring that vehicles were positioned properly for defensive measures. The day seemed normal until we started receiving small arms and sniper attacks from the semi-friendly buildings. I ordered all of the vehicles on the ground to engage the multiple targets in the buildings. My men on the ground would fire as well, ensuring proper defensive measures. Specialist Lafollette was with us on the ground that day. For most of the war up to the point of our engagements in Sadr, he had been behind the wheel of a vehicle, driving for everyone and watching his friends work on the ground and in the turrets of vehicles. James was an untapped resource. As good a driver as he was, he would have served a better purpose on the ground in the fight. On this day, I took him out with us so that he could stretch his legs. If anything should arise, he would defend his country on his own two feet instead of being separated from his weapon.

Every infantryman prepares for a fight, no matter what location, without the use of his weapon. I tried to give him the opportunity to be with his sword that day. He fought most valiantly and took back his pride. James did not need much coaching on the ground, surprisingly enough. All I had to do was give him one order, and he would execute the command with utmost haste. He stood vigilantly on security. When the first rounds were fired, he wavered not in his stance nor at his position. You could tell the anticipation for contact was high with this young, barley-hardened combat soldier. As the first round was fired toward us in hostile aggression, James looked back at me with a slight look of disbelief and confusion, much like you would see in the eyes of a child when attempting to face a new-found fear.

Upon seeing this, I calmly walked up to him and asked him a few simple questions. This was all that was needed with James. I said to him, "Do you see where the shots are coming from, up there in the top two windows of the three-story building? Do you see it?" I was trying to give him a little hint, give him some comfort that I, as a leader, was aware of what was going on and that he, as my brother-in-arms, was not alone in the situation.

He replied with a simple, "Yes, Sergeant, I do." I then smiled, patted him on the back, and told him the next time they shoot at us to engage the area. And if it happens again, he should keep engaging until the shooting stops.

He didn't need much guidance after this, because that was the only time throughout the day I remember having to talk to him. He did engage after that (a lot actually). I think at the end of three hours in contact, he had used up to 120 rounds. He was also still aching to stay in the fight, but he was needed back at the outpost. Men like James were the guys who made things worth coming out here: to give strength and courage to a brother, to let him know that when all hell breaks loose you will be right by his side through it all and that you won't abandon him regardless of how bad the conditions or situation may get or appear to get.

Captain Looney came to our side during the fight and engaged a third-story window with an AT-4 weapon. The commander and I were an excellent team on the ground. We never needed to talk to each other much, because we always seemed to know what the other was going to do next. In Special Forces you work closely with the team captain in order to benefit from a good working relationship. Usually, in the infantry, you do not see the commander on the ground with the men, and our working relationship made us more lethal.

Captain Looney came to my side with a rocket and asked where I wanted it. I told him to put it in the center floor of the building, because we kept seeing the least amount of firing coming from there. The logic was that because all of the shooting was coming from the top floor and none from the other levels, if we damaged the middle floor, we could block escape routes for the retreating enemy. There was also the possibility that they had weapons stashed or an aid station set up on a lower-level floor, and they were trying to draw our attention away from that area. I devised this plan because during the previous day, enemies were spotted in small groups entering and leaving this building and firing at friendly troops on the ground from the top floor. This plan worked, indeed, because after the middle story had been damaged badly by three 84mm AT-4 rockets, the enemy increased fire immensely for a few minutes.

We returned fire with equal ferocity, and after some time, the enemy stopped. Then silence took over, and a report came in that no enemy had left the building. The fire ceased after he launched the rocket, and we had again bought some time to work on the wall before the next attack. Suddenly, two RPGs impacted an Abrams that was providing security for our position, and to everyone's amazement, the vehicle stood as solid as it ever had been. The reason I say we were shocked on the ground is not because of how close the impact was. The men had been exposed to plenty of rockets already. The reason is because the enemy was using an RPG 29. You could tell from the sound and vibration of the explosion. This tank had little damage from the attack and would turn its fury on the insurgency.

A few more shots came in our direction, and then Schafer peered around a corner and noticed a man down the street taking a look at us with something on his back. Already having a grenade loaded in his weapon, Schafer shot toward the man, who was taking cover behind a wall and continually peeking out at us. His round impacted a broken-down motorcycle, which quickly exploded, and the man looked at us no more. Rockets and precision small arms fire started coming in from a nearby building perpendicular to the wall on the Sadr City side. Schafer engaged with more grenade rounds while everyone else took up exposed positions so as to engage the windows of the building.

After a few minutes of engagements and rounds being exchanged on both sides, Captain Looney ordered a cease fire because he'd had enough for one day. He called in an air strike with a hellfire missile. Two missiles impacted the building, and after that we received little to no contact in the area for the rest of the day. As the day turned to night, the enemy fortified positions in adjacent buildings to our ground location. They waited for the cover of

darkness and surrounded our position without us knowing, sneaky little bastards they were. It would seem that
all was going to be good for the night, and then it started
once again, kind of a like a farewell present from the insurgency: a final battle where it had all begun a month or
so ago.

The courageous forklift driver I spoke about earlier
drove close to the semi-friendly buildings and got stuck
on some wire. When I notified our team that the forklift was stuck about 50 meters south of our position, the
firing broke out. Everything got a bit more intense. We
were taking the usual barrage of RPG, sniper, AK, and
heavy machine gun fire. We were also pinned to a solid
location between the wall that we used for cover from
the attacks in Sadr City and the crane. Pinned like peanut butter and jelly between two slices of bread, we were
not going anywhere. Our only choice to really fight back,
besides firing with our own weapons, was to maneuver
the Bradley fighting vehicle and the Abrams battle tank
within 25 feet of our position.

Although this was a dangerous move, I had to use them
for protection, because as we would fire from the ground,
the enemy would only increase in their attack and in
number. I radioed to both crews on the ground that I
would have the men mark the buildings and ground locations from where we could see muzzle flashes coming,
and by our tracer rounds the vehicles could identify and
engage selected targets. At this time, our hearing protec-

tion was gone due to the hot day that brought along profuse sweating and much movement. In fact, it is a wonder as of today how I am still able to hear as well as I can. Both vehicles moved by our location, and as we began marking targets, they began engaging. The blasts, loudness, and constant concussion of the main guns made it hard to focus on reloading our weapons. It even became hard to communicate with radios; so we reverted back to old-fashioned hand-and-arm signals for communication.

The men began to fire and engage the enemy without talking or receiving guidance. Every man on the ground seemed to have his own area picked out and engaged it with a nearby brother of his. This was Payne's team from my squad, the same guys who were with me when I got hit in the neck. They split off in teams of two, so that when one man would empty a magazine and have to reload, he would step back a few feet and take a knee. This would be a signal for the second man to move up and accurately engage his target: not only to provide cover but to keep the enemy suppressed.

Reloading became difficult at times with the main guns firing from the armored vehicles. It's one thing in the daytime if you drop a magazine during a reload, because you can actually see it. At night you have the darkness, which makes everything confusing. In the military world, every good soldier knows that no matter how much you plan or rehearse something, when night falls the plan changes according to good ol' Murphy's Law. The firefight went on for about an hour until our air support came on station, and we guided them to the buildings where we had been taking all the enemy contact.

Once the missiles engaged the buildings, the fighting stopped. I looked around on the battle zone, and after weeks of work, all I could see was rubble and war for miles at a time. We had burned the city and crushed the enemy. What was to come of everything now? Peace between nations or more battles ahead? This was a battle that tested not only my leadership but a lot of other things as well. It was a test of patience, endurance, honor, and commitment, all of the things a man strives to test in his life. You never really know the level of how you scored in this test until others come up to you personally and tell you how much of an effect you had on them throughout the whole ordeal.

Later, it was official that during the night I had just described it really did become the last great battle in Baghdad for Sadr City. As I write this, it is a year later from the time when we started the battle, and all forces will soon be out of Iraq. This battle, as I suspected, turned young men who desired to destroy an enemy who would threaten freedom into honored patriots and protectors of their country. During all of the hot days and endless nights, these men stood their ground and never once faltered in the face of danger. This battle should be a lesson to all who would continue to oppose freedom in the future. Americans do not know how to fail when it comes to defending freedom, a love so great and a price so high that these men will still pay it gladly to this day. I will always be honored to know each and every soldier with whom I had the pleasure of working, regardless of past disagreements.

Now comes the time to speak of a friend who our platoon personally lost: Specialist Christopher Fox. Just prior to his death in September 2008, he was reassigned to our parent unit, Blackhawk Company, due to administrative reasons. He was a member of the Beaver Platoon, and that is how we will always remember him. Fox was out on patrol to an area north of our location in a different town. While handing a bottle of water to a little girl, Fox died when a sniper down an alleyway took a shot at him. The bullet penetrated his rib cage. He was flown home to be buried in Memphis, Arkansas. Giving a little girl a bottle of water: he was shot for doing a kind deed to a human being in need. This place can make you sick from many different reasons, but I think this had to be the worst. It's like a deadening sickness, one that makes your stomach go in a knot. You feel numb from hearing how one of your warrior brothers fell in this place, spending his final moments on the hot, dry streets of Baghdad. Fox fought with us through all the major battles while we were here in Iraq, and this is how it had to end for him. I can honestly say I am not sure of the details of his funeral. However, I can give you the details of how I found out about his loss.

It was my second morning at home in over ten months. I awoke when the sun was already up, went downstairs, and got a shower. Afterward, I turned the news on and sat back in a comfortable chair in front of the computer to check e-mail. I had a hot cup of coffee in hand and was about to take my first drink when the phone rang. It was a reporter from Fox's hometown in Memphis, Arkansas, who immediately asked me to comment on Christopher Fox.

At first I thought the kid had won some kind of medal, but it sank in within a second that this reporter was not calling to do a glory story about anything at all. Her voice had a saddened but cautious tone. As I realized this, she began to ask questions such as how well I knew him, how my relationship was with him, and what it was like to work with him. This made me quickly realize that I had no clue as to what had happened. She was the first to break the news to me of the incident. Her voice grew quiet, and she said, "Oh, no one has told you yet about what happened, have they?"

"No."

That was the only word I could mutter, because my voice had gone dry, and the worst thoughts of what could have happened already started running through my mind.

"Well," the reporter explained, "he was shot and mortally wounded by a sniper while handing a little girl a bottle of water. He was on patrol in Iraq on September 28 when

165

this happened."

My voice again was still dry; I told her that I appreciated the notification but had to go. I was in shock, but not like the shock from a firefight. It was the shock of loss. The reporter apologized once more and gave her sincerest condolences. I thanked her again and hung up the phone. Wanting something to make my mouth and throat not so dry, I drank from the coffee I had sitting there. It was cold. Have I been on the phone that long? I wondered. Or after hanging up the phone, did I just sit there in a state where all time passed me by unknowingly? The only judgment of time that I had during this experience was that my coffee was hot when I sat down and was about to drink it, and now it was cold. No matter how much I loved and missed my daughters, this one phone call most definitely put a damper on things for my entire time home, my only vacation that I would have in a year.

After a seventeen-day break at home in southern Indiana, the time was well spent with my daughters and the goodbyes once again were sad. When I was at the Louisville, Kentucky airport about to go through security and get on the plane, I was giving my final handshakes and hugs to family. When I was done, I turned and found my daughters to give them my goodbyes. They were each holding a single rose in hand. I knelt down and hugged both tightly and told them how much I loved them. Gabby told me her rose was for me to return back to her safely. Darby said her rose was a symbol of the love each of them had for me. I kept those roses through the rest of the deployment, and still today they sit on my dresser, looking as red as ever. To me those flowers are priceless: a gift from my daughters that will always be a remembrance of what I am fighting for in this world.

My sadness of leaving home would be replaced by the joy of being reunited with my brothers back at COP Ford. When I stepped foot inside the outpost, I was greeted randomly by the men who were carrying out their daily duties, the men with whom I had been serving all along. I quickly discovered later the first night I was back that there was something new about the attitudes of the men: everyone seemed to have more of a tight bond with each other. A picture of Fox was hanging above the doorway in our platoon bay area where we lived. There were letters posted from families and friends, saying how we were all heroes and were missed back home. The men seemed silent, yet more like family than I had seen them before. For me, this was closure. For me, this was when I saw the bond of brothers in combat once again.

11

TACTICAL
OPERATIONS CENTER

EVERY place in which a military unit operates has a Tactical Operations Center (TOC). COP Ford had a poor excuse for one when we arrived in Baghdad. The Command Post (CP) is the nerve center of all the operations conducted by the company. It contains the maps, computers, radios, and other technical and communications gear required to coordinate a unit's operations. The CP on Ford had the potential to be something that others would envy. When we arrived, the room we occupied from the 82nd contained a few collapsible tables, computers, and a map pinned to the wall. That was it, and I do mean it. Upon signing for the building, the company's first sergeant and the commander set out with haste to reconstruct the operations center. The company they led

168

was blessed with a number of experienced general contractors, carpenters, and others with construction experience. Thus, they began an immediate construction and renovation project to complete a productive and efficient operation center. For three weeks, you could not walk by the TOC without hearing a hammer pounding or a drill bit at work.

The effort encompassed a number of initiatives, including new walls, flooring, a raised platform, shelving, and electrical work, along with additional projects. The sergeants who were responsible for the work were exhausted, but they had taken plywood and built a masterpiece when the job was complete: something the Army would have paid thousands of dollars for an outside contractor to build. They had trouble with basic supplies; items such as screws and nails were not being supplied quickly enough by the military. So the men took it upon themselves to go out to the local markets and pick up what was needed.

This is how the unit operated: if the military could not help us, we would accomplish the mission ourselves ... even if it meant reaching into our own pockets. So what if there were people in the Iraq Theater of Operations earning three times as much while living in a better place than this? Who cares? Humble people get the job done without creating much of a fuss, and they are grateful for what they have. If you sit around all day and think about how much better everyone else's life is in comparison to

169

your own, it will only breed depression and bitterness. It will not allow you to accomplish what needs to be done for you to improve your current situation.

Meanwhile during the long days of fighting in the city, the phones in the TOC would ring nonstop. Sergeant Reinhart Larrea and Eric Carico would work the day shift, relaying the actions on the ground to higher command at battalion and brigade. At first, the higher command didn't take things seriously, which meant that getting authorization for an Air Weapons Team became a chore. Our air support during the battle played a vital role in our success, and a specific group of Apache attack helicopter pilots (call sign Long Knife 1-6 and 1-4) were our heroes throughout the entire battle. Other air elements supported us, but none would be able to match the drive and spirit these particular pilots possessed. The pilots would never question the authority or validity of the elements on the ground in regard to where a certain hostile target might be located. They would always engage what was asked of them, no matter who was on the ground.

When the fighting would cease for a momentary pause, Long Knife 1-6 would swoop down close to our position and fire flares to let the enemy know of their presence in the area and that our pilots were watching and waiting for the enemy's next move.

Not only did this have a demoralizing psychological effect on the enemy, but it provided a morale boost to all the men on the ground who felt alone in the battle.

It gave them a glimpse of hope during those dark days that they were not alone. Major Gossert, a strong leader and overall good man, always had our back no matter what echelon with which he would have to deal in regard to the higher chain of command. Major Gossert always saw that if the men on the ground were completing the mission, they needed the full support of the staff at their backs. He was the one who convinced the higher command at battalion and brigade to give Captain Looney full authority to call in air support at his own discretion. Without the major, our fight would have been far more difficult.

Certain ranks added stress to the daily operations at the TOC. When something would happen on the ground, Larrea would have to relay info to the battle captains at battalion. The responsibility of the battle captains was to get all of the information and report it to their higher chain of command in order to give more guidance and support for future missions. Our battalion's issue was having two men in the battle captain position who never spent time on the ground and could not fully comprehend the situation. For instance, when Larrea would pass word about an insurgent shooting from a window, the battle captains would want to know every detail about the man: what he was wearing, his grid location, and other information that could have waited.

Larrea's biggest problem was that while units on the ground would call over the radio and provide information about the insurgents we had sent to Allah, a barrage of information would follow. As a result, the battle captains would grow impatient at the higher level and often confuse or complicate things, instead of waiting for a full situation report (SITREP). Larrea decided to wait a few minutes after the incident and then send up information. He wasn't supposed to go this route, but he had no choice. He waited to hear if a man was shot, recorded the information, and waited patiently for confirmation that the target was neutralized.

The assessment of damage during a firefight only comes after the fighting has ceased, not during the actual shooting itself. Future commanders in combat should take note of this. If you are going to put men in charge of operations in the command center, then make sure they are competent enough to grasp the gravity of the situation and minimize stress in times of extreme combat. It makes sense to have a man do his hardship time on the ground during combat and then take a job with the higher command. He would be much more effective by possessing greater insight during combat situations, which can make everyone function as a stronger team.

AFTER BATTLE OPERATIONS

ONE memory I recall is when the men in this company had made a positive impact. In June 2008, Iraq had won a minor league soccer game against China. On that day, a party erupted in the streets. People were singing, dancing, and spraying silly string on the Humvees as we drove by. There was not one hint of a threat from the insurgency on that day, and everyone seemed to find joy in living in peace with each other. We were beckoned several times to step out of our vehicles and join in the festivities. Though it was tempting, we still had to maintain our posture and be ever watchful of our area. Nevertheless, this was one day that stood out in my memory as it showed me the comfort level the locals had with us being there.

The area that was assigned to the men of Steel Company was within the immediate vicinity of the outpost called Beida. It consisted of good people who wanted to maintain normal lives. They were mostly doctors, lawyers, and shop owners who never brought us much trouble (the trouble lay ahead in the days we spent in Sadr City). We didn't always fight in Baghdad. Sometimes, we just set out nightly and built rapport in our local area. Things eventually went back to a semi-normal state. Once again, we conducted patrols in our local neighborhoods to ensure safety and to keep the friendly relationship we had already established.

As the days passed, we became known as heroes in our area for defending the citizens from the threats of insurgency. We would be invited into their homes to sit and have tea and discuss issues within the area. Mostly, it was the same complaints about power outages, the heat, and the road conditions. Spending a few hours in town each day defined our role in the community. The children would always wave and ask us for candy, and a friendly neighborhood shopkeeper would cut us a deal on whatever we needed.

The schools, when in session, were always something to behold. Seeing the young children of this country dedicate themselves to something constructive rather than playing in the streets all day gave us hope for a better future. Our unit focused a lot on mini-projects for the schools, such as randomly stopping by to drop off backpacks and pencils for the children or fixing up a recreational area in the playground. This is one way we fought terrorism as well. If we could show the children we only had good intentions and meant them no harm, then maybe they could grow up to see the positive effects which had resulted from our actions. We all knew that the insurgency would be around during our generation. Doing things like improving local schools was something that was geared towards combating terrorism for future generations.

There would also be random stops at the CLC (Concerned Local Citizen) checkpoints, which were later referred to as the Sons of Iraq. CLCs were groups of ordinary people who wanted to protect their communities, and they garnered the support not only of our unit but of the entire U.S. military as well. They stood in groups of three to five men at road intersections 24 hours a day with nothing more than an AK and one or two full magazines of ammunition. It was always easy to work with them, and they were always quick to provide information about the area of town they were guarding.

A CLC would form multiple teams as its membership increased, establishing shifts and turning the operation into something of a 9-to-5 job for the citizens. This was not only a way for us to build up the local economy by offering jobs, but it also instilled patriotism in the men who worked the posts. Another benefit from the CLCs was that they kept local men in the area busy so that they would not be tempted to take up an offer from the insurgency to plant IEDs. That was an issue when we first came here.

The insurgency would seek out young men who didn't have work and give them a small sum of cash to plant an IED on a road, hoping that a convoy would drive by. We later learned that a man would not only get paid for planting an IED, but he could make more if the IED hit a significant target. An Abrams battle tank could fetch a large sum of money, and a Humvee would go for a little less. However, if a U.S. soldier was killed by an IED, that was top dollar in the bad guy market. That is why the employment of local men in the area was so important: it helped them to see a different side of things and kept them from getting caught up in a criminal element. These men started out with nothing at their posts but a little shred of hope and a weapon. Today, they have reinforced positions, plenty of help, and the respect of their communities. This is how Iraq is being rebuilt, and this is what the news does not tell you.

A few weeks after the fighting ended in Sadr City, our higher command saw fit to begin placing barriers everywhere in the city along major routes. They were under the impression that building the wall actually worked and that this is how we should fight terrorism. Actually, the wall itself was not the reason for our victory over the insurgency in Sadr City. Rather, it was our sheer display of U.S. firepower, which they had not seen since Fallujah in 2004.

When we were in Sadr, we let ordinary rules of engagement go out the window and replaced them with rules for pure survival, demonstrating once again what an infantry unit in the military can do with a single purpose. The intensity that the men brought to the fight over the course of 67 days made the insurgency think twice about launching rockets into the Green Zone or organizing small attacks on the outposts. No, the higher command said it was all due to the wall that was built. I personally feel that if we could have stayed in the city and given the people of Sadr an ultimatum to leave in a week or stay and fight, we would have found more insurgents and would have dealt a greater blow to terrorism in general. However, I am not in the position of authority to make such decisions. I am one who has witnessed what happens when the bigger kid on the block whoops the little kid in a street fight.

The men would get discouraged about having to go out into town to place barriers in what seemed like many endless nights to come. This time, there was neither contact nor fighting while the barrier operations commenced. Things were actually rather peaceful. We received a lot more support this time around as well. KBR even jumped in and gave us a hand for a time. I can recall one night when our platoon had been working barrier missions for a week and thought we were almost done until our higher command came down with a new plan to keep extending the barriers on certain routes. I gave this news to the men so that they could be aware that we were going to be working many long nights, most of which would not end until 4 a.m. That, in turn, would put us back to good ol' Ford at about 5 a.m. When I gave this news to them, they all had sad-kid-on-Christmas-morning faces. It was then that Hazelton jumped up on the table and said, "Now look! Did they give up when they stormed the beaches at Normandy? NO! Then we will not give up emplacing barriers!"

This lightened the mood, because everyone was laughing hysterically. It was all that the men, including me, could do. Home, at this point, was nothing more than a vivid memory and a distant vision. The days were growing hotter, and the nights were growing shorter. And hope was already at an all-time low. Laughter was about the only thing that would keep everyone going; so everyone became quite accustomed to making jokes about anything and everything, like the character from Napoleon Dynamite might say on a small poster "Heck yes, Iraq is pretty much the coolest place ever!" It was that kind of attitude you had to keep up in order to survive. The barrier missions eventually came to an end for us, and we went back into our communities to once again rebuild and protect them.

However, the enemy during this period had switched tactics on us. They knew that attacking us not only was dangerous but that it would lead to defeat. So they tried something else. They began by selecting individuals from the town who had authority in the community and would assassinate them in different ways. Some would be blown up in buildings at meetings or in their own homes, and some would be shot from a distance. This worried the community. Even though our lives were no longer directly threatened, that didn't mean we could let our guard down. As soldiers, we will always fight to defend freedom: not only our freedom but freedom for all. What the insurgency was doing was simply attacking freedom from a different angle.

After months of battle and low-key operations in the city, it would finally be time to transfer our equipment and responsibility to a new unit. By now, our vehicles were having major problems from all the wear and tear of daily missions in the city. I clearly remember on one of our last missions that the platoon was heading back to Ford at the end of the day. The vehicle I was in kept catching on fire from bad electrical work. The fumes quickly filled up the vehicle, and twice we were forced to abandon it out in the open—right at the edge of the city. Yes, there was a lot of work put into the great MRAP, but it still has its flaws today. In the end, we did the best we could with what we had for our final days in the sector while the new unit took our place. The new unit kept its guard down, and the enemy noticed.

After we returned to the United States, I was told that the men at Ford who replaced us were having their hands full. The enemy was toying with them. Sometimes in combat, you have to let people figure out what needs to be taken seriously. Always trust a man who has been in sector. Experience is invaluable, and heeding the voice of experience will save many lives. Eventually, two historians were sent to us by order of General Petraeus to get the real story of what had happened in Sadr City and put it in the National Archives in Washington, DC. They interviewed a few of us enough to confirm the story, to get details that had not been told, and to dispel rumors of what had happened. According to the historians, they had interviewed all of the units that were involved in building the wall.

All units, including every support element that took some small part in the operation but never helped us to engage or to destroy the enemy, were included in the interview project. You can only imagine my surprise and the surprise of the other men at Ford when we heard the historians tell us that all the other units (including the engineer unit that ran from the fight in the beginning) were solely responsible for building the wall. We had not even returned from deployment, and everyone else was claiming they had done all the work! Granted, there were eight battalion-sized elements that took part in this operation. Not one unit was responsible for the success of the mission. It was a collective effort. The main issue we had were with the people who had not fought but wanted the credit.

It was even said that the men who hauled the barriers down to a drop point near our location (not near the fighting, but a mile or so away) were taking all the credit and responsibility. When we showed the historians photos upon photos of our men at the wall, taking fire, and moving on courageously, they were taken aback. They continued with their interview, and upon their departure, they thanked us for all we had shared. It is my hope that they will do the story justice and preserve it in the National Archives for generations to come.

Tactics certainly did change as the days continued. Joint Security Station UR was hit with Iranian-made IRAM missiles that were launched from the back of a flat bed truck disguised as a truck carrying canned goods. The enemy would park the trucks a few hundred meters away from the base in a nearby alley in order not to be in direct line of sight with the base. They would set up and arm the rockets so that at the push of a button the rockets would launch into whatever base they were programmed to attack. By the time this happened, the triggerman could be long gone and out of sight. UR took a nice beating but no casualties. One squad leader on the ground that day, however, witnessed a rocket land within feet of where he was standing. As one rocket was shot overhead, the other rocket proceeded to skid on the ground and bounce a few times, giving the squad leader enough time to run for cover in a nearby bunker.

As each rocket came down from the air, they would detonate upon their second impact on the ground within a few seconds of impact. The enemy finally got a little smarter by using time-delayed fuses, but ultimately (and once again) their plan was met with failure because everyone would have enough time to reach safety. The confirmed damage reports stated that a few living quarters had been destroyed but nothing more. And, thank God, no one was in the living quarters at the time of impact.

Barrier missions continued off and on as our battalion would see order increase, chaos decrease, and new roads that needed to be blocked off to control traffic. On any given day, our company would be called to conduct raids on specified targets, and most of the time these raids would come with little or no notice to the men. As a platoon, we had to have our gear ready for any mission. All the men had to do was throw their boots on, walk out the door, and they would be ready to take on the city no matter what the task.

The last major raid we conducted for high value targets was in August 2008, when we captured two major leaders of the Hezbollah along with numerous insurgents. Our platoon was tasked with being the quick reaction force for the day; so if anything in the area happened, we had to be ready to go in a matter of minutes. This meant sleeping with boots on and having our gear close by. On a Sunday morning, I thought I would have a rare day off to relax as I went to the common area to get some food. No sooner had I just finished a plate of powdered eggs than Ullrich came into my room to tell me to get the men ready right away because we had been tasked to detain a few high-value targets. I should have saved those eggs for later.

I immediately grabbed the one man who had been with me every step of the way. Schafer had recently finished a four-hour guard shift and was dehydrated as all hell. The heat was around 120 degrees. He didn't drink much water that particular morning for reasons unknown and would regret it later. I informed him of the situation as he was walking in from his shift. He gave me a what- the-hell look, followed by obedience to the order I had given him. Schafer got the men up and out of their beds, and within fifteen minutes my squad, along with Ullrich, was in the four-gun trucks waiting for word to depart COP Ford.

We were told to get into the vehicles and start heading to a specific location. All information about the upcoming mission was passed along via radio on the way out to the site. The trucks moved faster than normal, as each driver was told that this was such a time-sensitive target that we had to get to the location within a matter of minutes. After ten minutes of driving fast through the labyrinth of a city, our platoon arrived on site to the designated location. As we pulled up, there was a moving truck backed next to the target house with items being loaded into it. Everyone jumped out before the vehicles came to a complete halt and rushed to stack on the main entrance door. They were two double, metal doors. Blake kicked the door in and immediately headed into the house, followed in suit by the rest of the men tasked for the mission.

There was shouting and screaming inside the house as people were brought out one by one. The women and children were kept separate from the men, because at this point we knew to detain everyone. Everyone was brought out of the house, and a detailed search was conducted of the building. Supplies for making IEDs were found inside the house in one of the upstairs rooms. Blake, Payne, Bryant, Schafer, and I went to the roof to gain access to the next building over. Payne injured himself by jumping over a wall on the roof, and Schafer had to bandage him up while I carried him downstairs to get looked at by our medic. Upon returning to the top of the roof, I spotted a man who was trying to hide by a door on the roof of the building next to us. It turned out that this guy would be the number two Hezbollah guy we were looking to detain.

The door he was trying to get into was locked from the inside, giving us a clue that someone had tried to escape and cover their route by locking a door to buy time. After busting the door down, Schafer, Blake, and I went through to the next house and ended up without support or any way of getting support. We went down the stairs and into the next house, where there was a man with his family. We went out to the alleyway and found all was empty; so we continued to search the area for weapons and additional men on our target list.

In the meantime, Captain Looney arrived on scene. His men immediately began maneuvering through the streets to catch the number one Hezbollah guy who had escaped from the alleyway that Schafer, Blake, and I were in. He was getting updates via UAV while running through the streets to where the lead Hezbollah guy was located. As soon as our vehicles had shown up on location, the lead bad guy took a route out of the alleyway and onto the main road. This was the reason the door on the rooftop was locked from the inside.

As Captain Looney and his men gained ground to the moving target, they came to a dead-end in the route. He knew that on the other side of the gate was a main road and that it was the only possible avenue of escape for the insurgent. Maybe, just maybe, the target had not passed by him yet, and with a little luck he might be able to get through the gate that blocked his route. His men were sweating profusely and breathing hard from running so fast through the streets. The lack of energy his small team experienced did not deter them from breaking through the gate.

With a few kicks to the door and one huge body slam, the gate busted open, and Captain Looney's team flooded into the street. Immediately and without knowing it, Captain Looney ordered the first car to be stopped and searched. To his surprise, the first car stopped was the car that was transporting the lead Hezbollah target. Looney was being filmed by an unmanned drone during the mission, and the live feed was used as a location marker of where his team was in accordance with our location at the house.

How this happened, I do not know. How we were able to hit one house and unknowingly have a second team intercept the target vehicle before it left the city for good is far beyond me. To me, this showed that the Almighty definitely had a hand in helping us on that particular day as he had done in the past so many times.

Though the standard of living and the focus of the men remained at high alert until the last days, the only comfort the men had was the near sight of home. Despite the loss of our comrades, this war changed every man for the better. We fought a war of great magnitude against an enemy who wanted nothing more than control of a people who had been oppressed for so long. We, as soldier

Beavers, stood our ground and did not waiver through-out the whole ordeal. This is how freedom is defended. This is how we as a nation will reign supreme and spread liberty for many generations to come.

There was always the problem of having a lot of leftover equipment that had to be turned in. The mechanics had to reconstruct a safe area so that they could avoid sniper fire while they worked. When our operations began, the mechanics were given the worst equipment with which to work. The vehicles were not mission-capable, yet people relied on the mechanics to have them up and running. Our mechanics felt almost helpless in the fight, because all operations would cease until broken machinery could be fixed. More direct contact was needed between the mechanics and the people who shipped the equipment parts. This remained a constant problem and was to blame for a lot of issues.

When our requests were sent from an outpost, they could get lost within the proper channels. When the battle started, the mechanics not only had guard duty on the COP, but they also had to continually work to keep the vehicles up to par. When operations started, vehicles were still not up to working standard. Potholes also caused problems for the mechanics, because once they got the vehicles working, they would have to do repair jobs almost continually. However, when a vehicle would come back badly damaged, the thought that went through the minds of the mechanics was not only fixing the vehicle but also concern for their brothers who were in it when the damage happened on the battlefield. This concern gave Bowden a chance to show skills as a mechanic and a motivation to make sure the vehicles were in top shape.

The mechanics felt a sense of accomplishment from their work, because they knew the soldiers depended on them as much as they depended on the medics when someone would get hurt. The infantry would fight, and the medics and mechanics would fix everything to get the process back on line. The deaths of Chris Simpson and Mike Elledge were the worst to fix. Not only was their vehicle smashed beyond repair, but they also had to look at the men who were with Simpson and Elledge when they died. It was a grueling experience, because the men who survived the attack went home soon after, but the mechanics would have to deal with the war-torn vehicle for two straight days, trying to recover it and retrieve the equipment. The effect took its toll on everyone from the basic rifleman to the company commander, but it fueled the energy of the men through the bloody war.

12

SUPPORT OF
THE FAMILIES

MANY at home wonder if they are ever doing enough—or what more they can do—to help the men and women who serve out here. All I can say is that you are doing enough, America. The support and outreach is overwhelming. I cannot begin to go into the many organizations that have been started with one particular goal in mind: to provide a small gift as a way of saying thank you. The people who support these organizations are the essence of America and are the reason soldiers of every race, creed, and gender come out here to willingly risk their lives.

Many think that America is taking a path in the wrong direction that will eventually lead to her demise. There really is a way to restore the faith of the American people: look at the example set by your sons and daughters who come here to fight for you daily. We servicemen and servicewomen believe in the Constitution of the United States and will defend it from all enemies foreign and domestic, so help us GOD. Every time you do a small act of kindness for a soldier in combat, you bless those around him or her. There is one organization called Fans4afghanistan that was started by a dear friend of mine, Shaliegh Schneider. Her husband and I went through the Special Forces course together and have been good friends ever since. She found out I was deployed. Instead of sending only a few electric fans, she sent one for each man in the Beaver Platoon. I was shocked at this gesture of support.

She had innumerable requests from soldiers and their families for these fans. But because she knew me personally, Shaliegh decided to put our platoon at the front of the line so that the boys could have a small comfort item. The fans arrived in four huge boxes, and the boys acted like it was Christmas all over again. When I brought them into one room and showed them the packages that had just arrived, you could see the happiness and appreciation on their faces. It was not only a gift that could beat the heat, but it was an act of kindness that made the men remember that freedom was worth fighting for. Sometimes that can be the most valuable gift of all.

My mother, Kathy Pirtle, was one person I could always depend on to come through, no matter what. At the time I was writing this book, gas was at a national average of $4 a gallon, and the economy was not doing so well (though it showed signs that it could recover in due time). Dear old mom made sure I would get a package with some oatmeal and soup in it every two weeks. I told her that I didn't want her to worry about sending things because of the economy. I wanted her to just save the money. What did dear old mom do? She kept sending boxes. My mother always felt that continual love and support would be my key to fight the good fight. It was her way of doing her part in the war as well. I can say to date that the most common item soldiers received were Girl Scout cookies. After all the years of missing out on them, I certainly did my share of catching up.

Niki Braxton of Greenville, North Carolina was a dear friend who always seemed to know the importance of the spiritual battle of a Christian during combat. She knew that all life is valuable, but what really mattered was the protection of the soul. She wanted to make sure I didn't lose my faith in the Lord. She did not send the ordinary day-to-day items necessary for living. What she did send had a very dramatic impact. She was proof of how the small things in life could matter so greatly. She sent a shield pendant to me on a chain with an engraving of a prayer on the back. It was a verse from Joshua 1:9 "Have I not commanded you? Be strong and courageous. Do not be afraid; do not be discouraged, for the Lord your God will be with you wherever you go." This verse gave me so much comfort and strength in some dire times during this war. At times, when our night operations reached a quiet point, I found myself pulling out the shield and reading it. After finding my strength, I would return to work. These are the things that help a soldier through war. Our bullets could only do so much in battle. Our underlying source of strength was ultimately our faith and the support we received from our loved ones.

Then there was Jack Morrison. Jack is a retired warrant officer who ran the Veterans Affairs Office in Rockport, Indiana for many years. Though he is my former father-in-law, even today Jack treats me as a son, and I view him as a father. He made sure that every two weeks I got something in the mail from him as a way of saying, "I've been there and know what it was like and want you to have something to make life comfortable." Jack is quite possibly the most unselfish person I have ever met, always willing to help out his fellow man. Jack served three tours in Vietnam with the infamous Black Horse, 11th Armored Cavalry Regiment. They dealt death to all who would oppose freedom; so I took a personal liking to them when I had first heard what it actually meant to serve with his unit. Even though I was divorced from the family, Jack showed me that there is a bond that stays with all men who serve in the military, especially in combat. For this I have the utmost respect for him.

Numerous church groups across America would continue to surprise me throughout my time in Iraq. Yes, they were doing their jobs as Christians, but the outreach and support from people I had never known was amazing. The boxes would always contain some sort of encouraging and grateful note about how prayers were being prayed for all of the soldiers fighting the war. These packages always brought a smile in the darkest of times, and I can tell you that the smallest things can make the biggest change in a soldier's day when facing an enemy whose only goal in life is to see you dead.

There are so many people to thank for the support we received. Many would send a simple care package or a movie, but it had a very positive effect. There is nothing like a handwritten letter, something made personally to an individual that in a way identifies his existence in a lost world of death and turmoil. Yes, the smallest things in life always did have the most positive influence on us.

In the end, my love for my daughters, Gabby and Darby, is why I fought in the Balkans War in Kosovo, in the invasion of Iraq in 2003, and in the Battle for Sadr City. I spent many days away from them each year that I was deployed. Even when I am back at my home base, Fort Carson, I only get to see them a few times during the year. But my absence does not change my love for them. I hope one day they will realize that fighting for them was the greatest gift I could give them. Time away from family takes a toll on a soldier, and it can never be recovered. I have missed the pleasure of seeing my daughters' sporting events and after-school activities. Knowing I did something to secure a safe future for my daughters is comforting to me. They are always in my thoughts and prayers.

13

The Personal Trial

It was hard to write about the battle while reliving it in my mind every day. I would be forced to recall each day, each incident, as if it were happening for the first time. As I awoke each morning from a dream about the battle, I would brush the distracting thoughts aside and start to write. This was another war: not one in which I fought to stay alive, but one I had to endure until it was told and off my chest.

The men had fought bravely throughout the ordeal, and someone had to make their story known. America would be proud of the things we did out in the streets of Sadr. We defeated terrorism on a very close and personal level. Politics had no room in the battles that raged in the streets, for it was man versus man and gun versus gun. It was who would be in the right place at the right time and who would take the bullet for the guy next to him.

This was not only a visible battle in Iraq; it was a battle for survival as well. In order to get the full story, I had to write while in Iraq before coming home. Often, I asked the men to relive their experiences. Something interesting happens when you ask your fellow soldier to recount the bloodiest day of his life. Not only does he tell you everything, but he also invites nearby friends to join in the conversation. I could see something in each man's eyes when I asked for a recount of the event that he remembered most, the one moment in combat that changed him. A long pause would often follow, along with a clasping of the hands.

Everyone seemed to grip his hands together as if looking for something to hold onto before recounting the major event in his life. The eyes would move from left to right while looking at the ground, searching for an answer that would justify individual actions while not looking weak. There was nothing to hide at COP Ford or after the battle. Every man seemed to face his own personal demons and to conquer them. Out of nowhere, the story would start, and the soldier would speak. The soul would pour out memories as each man would recount personal experiences step by step, making sure to disclose all information. The little things a person can remember about life-changing events always surprised me the most.

Many times, a soldier would remember the temperature or if he had just finished the last bit of warm water from his canteen or if the sweat was so bad it would seep into his eyes, making it almost impossible to see for a few minutes. It was hard enough to sit down and talk with one guy. Asking about 100 soldiers to tell me about their time in war so I could do justice to our story was the hardest part.

My journey with Christ is something I could literally write another book on. Instead, I will hit on the key points of what helped to strengthen my faith in the Lord. As you have read, I witnessed many miracles during the Battle of Sadr City. Miracle is the only word I can come up with to explain how such violence ensued and how heroic actions by a few would save the lives of many. Sniper shots coming within inches of my head, IEDs not exploding until after I walked by, praying the rosary only to see prayers answered the same day, taking shrapnel to the neck and having the sliver of metal come within millimeters of the jugular vein ... I consider all of these miracles. We could have lost a lot more men to the battle given the circumstances and the odds.

Take Private Nathon Bagwell, for example. He was on the wall unhooking the crane and took a direct hit to the abdomen from a sniper, a 7.62 mm caliber. A round of 7.62 mm does not just enter the body. As it penetrates, it takes the path of least resistance, making the bullet bounce around and causing damage. It travels along major arteries and veins until reaching a major organ or exit point. It could enter the foot and exit the shoulder. In Bagwell's case, it went through his abdomen, ricocheting off the edge of his hip (iliac crest) and exiting his back. He still suffers injuries to this day and may never fully recover. But he made it out with his life.

There is also something about a life-and-death situation that encourages sarcasm. I read an article somewhere that sarcasm is now a considered a type of survival mechanism. While Bagwell was lying on the stretcher and the PA was evaluating him and beginning treatment, Bagwell grabbed the PA by the shoulder, pulled him close, and said, "Tell her I love her."

"Who?" the PA responded.

"I don't know. I just always wanted to say that in a situation like this."

This brief exchange made everyone in the operating room crack up. Men do things like this when they are faced with uncertain fates in unknown situations. It's a way of adapting to stress.

It was not only sarcasm that helped one to survive battle, but faith as well. If you don't have faith in God, have it in something. In battle, you feel like you are a prisoner. You are confined to a certain area with rules and regulations. You do not know if you will ever leave the place you are in. I remember a story I read during the battle that inspired my faith. This story helped me to hold fast to my beliefs and fueled hope. Richard Wurmbrand was imprisoned in Russia for preaching about Christ in 1948. The one thing I took away from his story was that in the worst of situations, being beaten and tortured daily, he learned to love his enemies so that he could see them through God's eyes and not his own. When his captors would beat him daily, he didn't focus on the pain or the methods they used to torture him. Instead, he focused on how to better love and forgive his captors. He would later go on to recount that when the beatings would go on daily, he no longer felt pain but rather saw angels surrounding him. All he could feel was love and pity for his captors in spite of what they were doing. They didn't have a particular hatred for Richard himself. The captors did what they did because they were made to believe that he was the one in the wrong.

How blind do all of us become to the things we think are right when they are actually wrong? Drinking, drugs, sex addictions, and squandering your time instead of honoring God with it are choices we think will have little or no consequences. But they actually have far greater consequences than we can fathom. So whenever you are faced with the question of which road to travel, my best advice to you is to consult Paul's first letter to the Corinthians. He lays down all the basic guidelines for living a good life, and on top of that he tells you of the weapons with which you must be equipped in order to win the spiritual battle in life. They are metaphors, but with a little study you can understand fully what Paul is trying to say. One thing to note is that he never speaks of any armor for your back. In a battle, God does not intend for us to run away from the enemy. He expects us to stand and fight.

If you run away from the enemy, you are exposed and weak. An example would be not facing a major sin in your life so that you let it rule over you.

Some will say that all people are evil by nature, and it is true. All people are capable of evil deeds. However, all people are equally capable of very good, wondrous, remarkable deeds as well. It is not for us to judge the enemy. We are made to forgive each other and not let bitterness grow in our hearts. When bitterness grows in a person's heart, the result is war, treason, rape, murder, and all kinds of detestable things. If we forgive, then we gain insight into the heart of evil. We will then begin to see through the eyes of the Father in heaven and not through the eyes of man. It is true that Satan has the keys to this world, but in no way does he have the keys to the next or to the hearts of man.

Writing this book brought a sense of peace and a place I could escape from the madness of war. Many times, I would find myself staying up very late with little or no sleep before the next patrol, because there was a comfort that came with telling this story. This was another way to stay connected to home. Anything you could do during war to stay connected to home was as precious as blood, because if you didn't, you chanced growing distant from the world itself.

In conclusion, no matter how hard or miserable life may be, always remember there are small victories to be won. Once you start winning the small victories in life, you can go for the bigger ones ... and that can only lead you to greater things down the road. Trust in the Lord, for he will guide you. It is good to have religion, but don't put more faith in your religion than you do in the Lord. You were made to live a full life, and in this life there is much fullness to be found.

14

A Soldier's Thoughts
(A special thanks to SFC Jacob Gomez for this chapter)

IT is surprising how much a man can learn while he is in an area, isolated from his loved ones at home. Iraq has a way of making a man think hard about weaknesses. Only when the weak areas are realized and assessed can a person begin to undergo transformation. Iraq will either make or break a man, turning one for the better or the worse. We had a few soldiers who deployed with us only to return home within months because they were not strong enough to tolerate daily life in Iraq.

Our platoon had one guy who received a minor injury while he was sitting in the turret of a vehicle. He used this injury to claim a number of illnesses so that he could go back home to his girl, only to discover that his girl thought his actions were disrespectful to the men over in Iraq. So she left him.

Men like this do not deserve to wear the uniform of a soldier. In fact, they give soldiers in general a bad reputation. I am not saying by any means that Team Steel or Charlie Company stands as the best combat unit ever to walk the face of the earth. Our soldiers had many faults as well. What I am saying is that no one who has been through the entire conflict, returned home to a different war, and gone back again can understand what can compel a soldier to leave his comrades in the middle of combat. This is as bad as treason itself, an offense that used to be punishable by many hours of beatings or even death. Some would say that after graduating basic training and seeing regular Army life, they suffered from pre-traumatic stress.

You've got to be kidding me.

This kid only served a month in the Army. Prior to arriving in Iraq, I had to out-process him from the Army. His reason for being unstable was pathetic at best. I remember clearly the details of this time, because I spent the last two weeks I had in America taking care of this soldier and getting him out of the Army along with another soldier who had an addiction problem.

I could understand the third soldier a little better, for he served his time already in this war. The nightmares were too much to handle. So he turned to drinking. I had done this at one point in my life and discovered that this was not the answer to anything. Christ is where the answer is and always will be. In the end, we all have our demons to face, whether they are in a foreign country in time of war or at home with our family and friends. These personal demons arise in all of us. It is how we engage these demons that determines if we will let them ruin our lives or if we will defeat them.

To defeat the enemy within, you must first recognize and study it: assess, strategize, and implement a plan. If you think nothing in the world can bring you down, you are certainly destined for failure. The hardest part about becoming a better person often is a long, hard look in the mirror. The funny thing about war is that you take a long, hard look at yourself daily, sometimes not wanting to see what is staring right back at you. But you look, nevertheless. In war you have to compare yourself to your enemy and gain a firm grip of what you are up against so that you can avoid defeat. You need to study his every move as if it were a game of chess. Never underestimate him nor anticipate the next action. To do so will only invite defeat.

COP Ford had a way with a man's mind. I believe it was the solitude that emanated from this dark place which produced despair in great measure. There were many other soldiers at the base, yes, but it was a different kind of loneliness that one endured. You often had to encounter the loneliness that truth can bring, and for some that can be the most isolating thing on earth. All of us are born with faults. When we begin to deny or cover up our faults, we become weak. Baghdad did not allow for weakness, and neither did Sadr City. So you only had one option: to become strong wherever it was that you were weak.

The worst thing about weakness is the initial realization that you are actually vulnerable to something. It's sickening to the stomach. For example, the first time you get shot at, your knees buckle, your pulse races, and you search for a place to run. But this only lasts for a second, because you realize that if you're going to get home alive, you must destroy or at least force the bad guy to run away. To get to this mind-set and to train your body to do these actions requires anger, not fear.

The men at COP Ford with whom I talked felt the same way about taking fire from the enemy. The first round that went by a man's head during our gun battles was followed by initial fear that was quickly turned to anger, and the anger did not leave. If anyone ever tells you that the first time they were shot at, they immediately became angry, I would call that man a liar.

Getting shot at is not a natural thing; so it takes fear to realize what is happening. Then it takes anger to conquer it. I'm not saying that the men ran in fear. The fear-to-anger transition would happen within a few short seconds, but it would seem as though they were some of the longest seconds of a man's life. The fear would only stay around initially. Every time after a shot is heard, the only emotion known is anger. I think it is more of a survival instinct than anything else. That is why the men fought boldly.

The first time I was shot at was during the invasion in 2003, prior to the capture of Baghdad when my unit was in the holy city of Najaf. My squad of eight men was surrounded by a group of militia. Rounds continuously rained down on our positions along with numerous RPGs. I remember hitting the sand and not wanting to be there. I also remember getting up a few seconds later and running through the hail of bullets to pull a buddy of mine out of the concertina wire he was caught in. (This was the story I spoke about earlier where Kyle got stuck in the wire.)

I remember not being afraid to fight back from that moment on. It all came back to me in Sadr City: fear not having a place in my emotions. I just looked for the enemy and returned aggression. This was a blessing in a way, because as a leader I saw the initial reaction of my men, which was the same reaction I had years ago. I showed my men that there was nothing to fear by immediately returning fire upon the enemy. I not only gained their respect, but I instilled courage in them as well. My men became noble warriors for freedom and justice.

There is truth in the age-old saying that there are no atheists in foxholes. Every man out there found his own God to whom he would pray, and pray each did. Exactly how does one go from being on a constant adrenaline rush while putting his life on the line to being back in his quarters with only his thoughts to himself? This all happens within an hour, maybe less. How does one deal with a daily transition like this? Every soldier deals with war in a different way. Some keep to themselves and read. Some laugh and make jokes so that they can forget about the reality of the situation for a short period.

It is not easy to be out in a town where everyone hates you and wants to kill you one minute to being back in the safety of your room the next. I have had personal demons surface in a cell-like room: remorse about things I had done many years ago. Memories I have no way of correcting, and can't seem to erase, are the source of an internal struggle. Spiritual battles constantly rage in my soul, because I began to feel like I was playing God by taking others' lives. This forced me to wonder if all the people I had killed were really bad people and how many innocent lives I might be responsible for taking. I can recount numerous times on the streets of Sadr City when I had been given the order to open fire on a building from where we were taking contact.

I still entertain the thought that there could have been small children in those locations. How many innocent people must pay for the cost of freedom? How many more will die out here because of the lack of solid information? How many entire families or generations of families am I accountable for wiping out completely? These are the thoughts I live with daily, and the tears I shed on a cold Friday night are for them.

This leads to thoughts of my own family back home. Do

they really know what kind of a monster I have become in this environment, and will I return the same person whom everyone remembers and loves? No matter how many times my mother or father may say that they love me and are proud of me, it is hard to convince myself that this is true after what has happened. How will my children look at me when they are older and find out the things I did?

When I set out to serve my country, I was trained to defend my fellow soldiers and myself. However, no training could prepare me to deal with taking lives of innocent civilians. I have many nightmares about this, and sometimes they get so bad I can actually see the faces of the dead in my dreams. As a leader in combat, I have drawn strength from the Lord Jesus and his Blessed Mother. I know what forgiveness is, and I do my best to forgive others since I have made my share of mistakes. A person can tell me a hundred times that I did the right thing, but the question remains whether I could have done something to prevent a specific incident.

Silence on occasion would hit and stop me in my tracks. When the patrols and combat first started, my soldiers would often joke around on the way out to the area of operation. They did this to alleviate the stress and tension created by the prior day's events. The joking slowly faded after the violence picked up, and the boys would remain silent on the way out to the city, heading for a fight. Every soldier sitting in the transport vehicle would keep to his own thoughts, wondering a million things and enjoying his only possible moments of peace for that day.

Not one soldier would break the silence, because that would mean you were the weaker person. No one wanted to acknowledge weakness, thereby making himself vulnerable and incapable of completing the mission at hand. In time we would all come to realize that the silence was a source of strength for the battle.

For a number of our leaders, some of the decisions made by the higher command were hard for us to deal with. The men saw that we were the ones on the ground doing all of the fighting and had the best view of what was going on. Soldiers on the ground who built the wall in Sadr City and shed blood for our country felt that we were in a position to make decisions on how to conduct the mission. Yes, we will always need intelligence reports and documentation, but the soldier on the ground is the most useful source of information.

One event that was really hard on a great leader in our company occurred when Private Nathon Bagwell had taken a shot to his abdomen. As Bagwell was unhooking a crane from atop the wall, the officer in charge had adjusted security and taken all the correct measures to ensure his safety. But regardless of his authority and the precautions he ordered, he felt utter helplessness to prevent Bagwell from being shot. This particular leader was on top of his game at all times, but in this instance he could not help but feel that he had failed. He felt that he had not done enough as a leader. He truly modeled a high standard of leadership by readily accepting responsibility for what happened to the men who fought bravely next to him.

As soldiers, our emotions and thoughts were suppressed day after day due to the intensity of our involvement in the operations. Downtime played havoc with our emotions, and many of us began reflecting on why we were tasked to build the wall in Sadr City. Did it really make sense to build a wall? Will it succeed? Only time can tell.

The instantaneousness of the actions on the ground dictated how soldiers and leaders reacted to a situation at any moment. People say perception is reality; so whose reality are we to believe: the leaders up higher, resting in the comfort of their secure headquarters, or the soldiers who were fighting and sacrificing to execute their intent?

The Battle for Sadr City was not your classic battle, featuring tank-on-tank or man-on-man combat. The soldier in this case always found himself fighting on a variety of fronts. This is what made the men of Team Steel, 1-2 SCR, and 1-6, along with all other soldiers in the battle space so great. No matter what the task was, we certainly would make it happen. That became a kind of unspoken motto for future missions among all units involved. When a mission would come down that seemed pointless and we were given minimal men and below-standard equipment to accomplish the task, we would always say, "Don't worry, America; we'll make it happen." And we did make it happen. We did everything and anything our country asked us to do.

Regardless of perspective, there came a time in war when enough was enough. On June 7, 2008, Lieutenant Galen Peterson of Blue Platoon was exposed to his seventh IED blast. Peterson was an outstanding and reliable leader, one to whom his men could relate. He carried a boyish look on him that spelled friendship and kindness to everyone he met, always passing you with a smile. You never really heard a mean word come out of his mouth against anyone. No, Peterson just loved life, and he loved being a patriot for his country. One too many times he was exposed to an explosive blast that was meant to rip through a tank. He took all the others like a champ, but the last one shook him to his core. When he got medevac'd, he was asked if he knew where he was. He replied, "No, but it snowed today." Snowing? It's snowing? What do you say when you hear that one of your brothers got hit so hard he thinks he is in Siberia?

Nothing.

You don't say anything. However, you do think to yourself about how sad the situation is. He was guarding a wall that had yet to serve a purpose. When he was brought into the aid station, the early reports came back that he was going to be okay. How could he be okay? This guy had earned his ticket home with lucky number seven; so how could he be all right? He will always have to live with the side effects of all of the concussions he suffered over the past few months. They will forever be a part of who he is.

The side effects from combat are wounds of war that are hardly possible to heal. Word finally came down an hour or so later that he would be leaving us. He would be getting a medical evacuation to another area out of the immediate combat zone where he would receive further treatment and a diagnosis of future problems he may encounter.

The Army loses a lot of men like Galen Peterson who would have freely given his life for the country and the cause. They lose men like him because bad men do bad things to good people, and Peterson would be there stop them. Soldiers of less caliber in this war often complained of false injuries and were sent home as heroes. Peterson undoubtedly went home a hero, but it will add to his wounds when he hears of a soldier going to Iraq, faking an injury, returning home, and claiming the same benefits he received. That is a disgrace, and the men who have seen the horrors of war and have endured endless hours on patrol know it is a battle they will have to face later. It's not a battle involving the enemy with AKs and RPGs. Rather, it is a battle of mixed emotions that only the Lord could help one win.

I found that the Lord puts us through trials and tough times in life in order to make us stronger and to bring us to the full potential of what He created us for. The Lord brought all of us at COP Ford this far. He will see each one of us through until the end. If there is one thing the Lord is truly known for throughout all the ages, it is warfare. He is a God of love and peace, but he truly understands the costs of that freedom and the ongoing battle of good versus evil. The devil struck us often in Baghdad, but the Lord has not yet abandoned any one of us. Even the three dear brothers of ours who were taken home served as a necessary driving force that got all of us through on a daily basis.

Surely the Lord will not take anything from you in this life that he will not give you back tenfold either in this life or the next. I also told the men quite frequently to take heart and know two good things about being in Iraq: either you die in Iraq and go home to our Father in heaven or you survive and go home to your loved ones with a greater respect for them and for life in general. So it is a win-win situation, no matter how you look at it. You either go home or you go home. This is the mindset I kept every day of the heavy fighting. My faith did more to keep me alive than my training ever could have, and I owe it all to the Lord.

The trials on the battlefield resemble the struggles everyone deals with daily. The healing from my divorce was my biggest demon. I am not hurt over my ex-wife, but I feel I had in some way failed my daughters, whom I love dearly. Many people are hurt by divorce. The hurt typically results from words that are said in the beginning and later regretted. I was divorced long ago, and I vowed not to say anything I would regret against my ex-wife. So I offer this bit of advice to those who are experiencing the pain of divorce: it is OK to compromise to reach agreement on issues for the sake of the children involved.

If you have lost something in your life, and you know it was lost because you let it go, then stand up and take back what is yours. Keep family close, and keep the Lord of Heaven above everything. He will guide you through all times of trouble and never abandon you. When things seem at their worst in your life and you feel you are all alone, that is when you must fight hardest. Just remember that the Lord will not leave you alone. Do not think you must go into this battle with no one to support you. He made you, and he loves you. The Lord will not forsake you.

Visits home during wartime are ironically quite difficult. First, I didn't want to leave my brothers in Sadr City. Second, it is difficult to keep in the back of my mind that I have more time to serve in the war after the visit is over. It's depressing to think about, and all I can do is look forward to the day when I will actually be home and done with the war. The night before I had to get on my flight and go back to the war was particularly difficult. I wondered if there was something more I could have done during my vacation to make the time go slower. I read to my daughters every night and spent every moment I could with them.

A short vacation in September 2008 was an especially

difficult break for me. While I was home, I was notified of a death in the family. A few days later, I was told that Fox was shot and killed by a sniper. Two more deaths followed while I was at home, and I can honestly say that it was not the dream vacation I thought it was going to be. I had been looking forward to coming home and relaxing, but the vacation turned out to be a time of mourning. I suppose it was better to hear all the bad news while I was at home so that I could be with the families involved and comfort them rather than reading about it in a foreign country in an e-mail.

One blessing I experienced during this visit was a brief stay at Saint Meinrad Archabbey, which is located in my hometown of St. Meinrad, Indiana. The Archabbey is a jewel in southern Indiana. I went up there for a few days and just walked around, looking at the Lord's handiwork. During my stay, I found peace with the war and myself. I came to terms with everything bad that had happened during my two deployments in Iraq. My priest, Fr. Jeremy King, OSB, talked with me and helped make sense of the chaos I was experiencing in my mind. He assured me I should not feel guilty about anything that happened in battle. Since I did my job and did not take things into my own hands for personal gain, no guilt remains. Anger is what I should feel. Anger is good, because it is a lot healthier than carrying guilt around with me. Guilt would only bring me down, and it does not go away. Anger eventually subsides, and in this instance I was in the right for being angry. Jeremy also said that God sends us angels in life; so in turn I should go out and be an angel for someone else. This could serve as a penance for my sins.

The monastery had a peace that I cannot describe. It was as if just being there in the presence of the Lord was able to heal me from the inside. This is why I continually say that Christ is where the answer is. Sometimes you will not know that He is the answer, or you might never get an explanation. But have faith that He is. Healing can be found when you submit to the Lord and begin to serve others and not yourself. After all, that is what Jesus did when He came to earth. He was here to serve us, not rule us. So in conclusion, why despair in your sufferings in life? The Lord has already suffered for us on the cross. Look to that when you are in the dark hours of your life, and you will find hope.

God bless, and Godspeed.

15
AFTER ACTION REPORT
(by Command Sergeant Major John A. Kurak)

THE 1st Combined Arms Battalion, 68th Armor Regiment (1-68 CAB) deployed under the command of the 3rd Brigade Combat Team (3BCT), 4th Infantry Division in support of Operation Iraqi Freedom 07-09 (OIF 07-09) in December 2007.

1-68 CAB (Silver Lions) established operations from FOB Taji and conducted a relief in place with 4-9 Infantry, 4th Brigade, 2D Infantry Division. After completing an initial reconnaissance of the area of operations in January 2008, the Silver Lions initiated a COIN-oriented campaign plan in January 2008. The campaign plan was to ensure a smooth transition of battle space and continue the progress and transition of security, markets, and governance by leveraging the full spectrum of resources and support of 1-68 CAB to influence the areas within the Istiqlal Qada, and to disrupt and defeat active AIF within the LION OE with precision lethal and non-lethal targeting.

In a time period covering January 2008 through the end of February 2008, 1-68 CAB engaged with local leaders, building relationships to help influence the relevance of the government of Iraq (GOI) through local Nahia meetings and the Istiqlal Qada meeting. The Silver Lions began lethal precision targeting against JAM SG and AQI elements. As the Silver Lions conducted daily operations, they focused on building the local Iraqi Police from the Al-Zahour Security District, and the 5th Special Troops Company.

The Silver Lions conducted reconnaissance under the initial campaign plan, Silver Lions Footprint. The reconnaissance was focused on identifying projects that would increase economic development, improve government-provided services to the people, and develop intelligence on local criminal and AIF activities. Our battle space consisted of both Sunni and Shia divided predominantly by ASR Dover. The Sunni communities were on the west side of our sector, and the Shia communities were mainly to the east. The Sunni communities were mainly agrarian, and the Shia communities focused more on markets and industry.

The Shia communities within our sector were mainly Hussnaiyah, and Boob-Al-Sham. The main Sunni communities were Rashidiya and Fahama. The battalion

217

commander (LTC Michael Pappal) focused his unit on developing local infrastructure and enabling the GOI and ISF. Throughout the initial phase, the battalion developed TTPS on precision targeting and began to patrol in areas that the previous unit could not go. Subak Sur (Saba Qusar) was controlled by E Company but had not seen coalition forces in many years. It was determined to be a rather large community that had ties to Sadr City and the Adamiyah NAC, but it was also linked to Hussnaiyah/Boob-Al-Sham through the transportation of accelerants. Fahama was another enclave that the previous unit was unable to patrol.

The battalion began a campaign to disrupt criminal activity and deny the enemy the ability to emplace IEDs. D/1-68 (commanded by CPT Kevin Kahre) conducted Operation Safe Roads by emplacing concrete barriers along Route Dover to deny enemy engagement areas. The wall started at the southern end of Boob-Al- Sham and continued up to the first main intersection. This obstacle denied the enemy the ability to affect operations and provided CF freedom to maneuver. Another effort for the operation was to purge corrupt IPs from the Boob-Al-Sham Station.

D/1-68 arrested three IPs and maintained surveillance on a fourth officer for future operations. With the help of the local police chief, the chairman of the council, and other people in the community, they were able to get the intelligence we needed to identify and target the criminal and terrorist elements working in our district. We arrested 3 members of the local police who were responsible for murders and helping the local IED cells.

We conducted a joint operation with the local police and national police to search the factory area of Boob-al-Sham. Our search yielded 3 different caches spread across the town containing rockets, mortars, explosives, RPGs, and other munitions that would have been used against coalition forces and the Iraqi security forces. They conducted many other operations and raids resulting in the detention of over 20 terrorist fighters and criminals. All of these actions combined have greatly improved the security of this district. At the same time, they also brought much needed relief to the people of Boob-al-Sham.

On February 9, we conducted a medical operation at a local school that treated close to 250 people with a huge range of ailments from cancer to the common cold. They worked closely with our civil affairs team to help build new schools and clinics in this area. The focus was to help the local councils and government of Baghdad to provide these services and relief using their own systems and funds. This was the permanent solution that all coalition forces in Iraq were working to achieve, to get the local governments able to solve these problems for their people.

C/1-68 (commanded by CPT Todd Looney) was assigned Rashidiya as his initial battle space. This was a Sunni community that was semi permissive to coalition forces.

Initially, Team Steel conducted a relief in place, transition of authority with A/2-12 Field Artillery for the Rashidiya Area of Operations. Rashidiya Nahia consisted of the population center of Sabah Al-Nisan.

The main spheres of influence (SOL) contacts were Sa'id Ishmael, Sheikh Mohan, and General Mish'an. During Team Steel's time in Rashidiya, their main achievements were the registration of 373 members of the Concerned Local Citizens (CLC) of Rashidiya at 12 CLC checkpoints, paying nearly $140,000 to CLC members for their participation in the program, and also the introduction of several micro-grants and micro-generation electricity co-op programs. During their stay in Rashidiya Nahia, Team Steel was in small arms contact with anti-Iraqi forces (AIF) near a CLC checkpoint along the main route in Rashidiya on January 21, 2008. While in contact, Steel soldiers acted accordingly and drove off AIF before they could seize or overrun the CLC checkpoint.

B/1-68 (commanded by CPT Matt Jensen) was assigned the area of Hussaniyah and the responsibility to secure and operate the Joint Security Station-Istiqlal (JSS-I). They coordinated with the Al-Zahour security district and the 7th Special Troops Company of the Iraqi Army. B/1-68 initially deployed two platoons to operate/secure the facility and to conduct operations in the area. In the first operation, OPERATION BLACKHAWK MEGAN I, B/1-68 received intelligence from an adjacent unit, 2-325

AIR.

They captured a high value target, who was implicated in the IRAM attack on COP Callahan. B/1-68 quickly became the link between Istiqlal and the battalion. They played a major role in conducting the Al-Zahour District Security Meeting and the Istiqlal Qada meeting. B/1-68 was a major influence within the Qada.

E/1-68 (commanded by CPT Brian Soule) reorganized his from a two-platoon engineer company into three engineer line platoons, a maintenance team, and the company headquarters. Upon arrival in Iraq, the platoons attended the Task Force Iron Claw Academy, becoming fully qualified to conduct route clearance missions in Iraq. Following this training, 1st Platoon was sent to the operational control of 237th Engineer Company for route clearance missions. 1st Platoon conducted relief in place (RIP) training with 237th and assumed control for autonomous route clearance patrols on 25 January 2008, focusing on the Adamiyah District of Baghdad and the Istiqlal Qada of Baghdad. The remainder of Easy Company conducted a non-standard RIP with A/2-12 Field Artillery for the Subak Sur area of operations.

Since no coalition forces had operated in Subak Sur on a regular basis for two years, their primary mission was to conduct area reconnaissance and population reconnaissance to increase situational awareness of the new area of operations.

HHC/1-68 (commanded by Enardo Collazo) was assigned the region of Fahama. The area is part of the Adamiyah NAC, but due to the rural nature of the area had never been represented at that body of government. HHC/1-68 first conducted a MEDCAP to allow the unit the opportunity to assess the community. Fahama is a poor rural farming community with remnants of AQI establishing bed-down locations. HHC/1- 68 was a non-standard mission that allowed the battalion to focus on each of the vital locations within the LION OE.

F/1-68 (commanded by CPT Regan Allen) initially focused on the establishing the battalion footprint at Camp Taji, and would transition to the sustainment mission for JSS-I. F/1- 68 would begin looking towards the battalion's next mission set south of Istiqlal into the area referred to as Sha'ab, by providing sustainment pushes to COP Callahan and 2-325 AIR.

Offensive operations for the battalion were focused on SIGINT targeting of key special group individuals in Hussnaiyah, Boob-Al-Sham, and AQI targets in Fahama. An early operation for the battalion was LION Black. The operation was to coordinate B/1-68 conducting a SIGINT search with D/1-68 providing blocking positions in the event the target became dynamic. This became a weekly brigade-directed event. The target, though, incurred a motorcycle accident and left to Iran for surgery. The battalion continued to learn key lessons for SIGINT raids, catching a 2-25Brigade high value individual or (HVI), a 3-4 HBCT HVI and three battalion HVIs.

Towards the end of the first quarter, we received orders to assume the additional battle space of Sha'ab. As part of the RIP with 2-325 AIR, the battalion cross-attached C/1-68 to the White Falcon to decrease the disruption of combat operations.

C/1-68 would assume force protection and operate out of COP Ford. The battalion began conducting joint operations with the White Falcons to increase our familiarization of our new battle space. The first operation was Operation Greenwood to disrupt special group operations in Saba Qusar. D/1-68 was task organized with two tank platoons (truck mounted) and an engineer platoon. D/1-68 conducted over twenty-three cordon and searches of residential buildings and detained seven mid-level Special Groups criminals who were processed to Camp Cropper Detainment Facility.

The second quarter of our operations began with the battalion completing RIP with 2-325 AIR and assuming additional battle space and movement of our battalion HQs from Camp Taji to COP Callahan. Our battalion OE would incorporate Sha'ab, Beida, Ur, Basateen, and our previous OE of Istiqlal. With the additional battle space, we reorganized all of our subordinate companies to include our Forward Support Company (FSC) to allow them the capability to become landowners.

F/ 1-68 was task organized with scouts and snipers to allow the FSC the ability to conduct sustainment operations and force protection operations for COP Callahan.

The former used two separate companies to accomplish this with a ground reconnaissance troop for external protection and their FSC for internal force protection. F/1-68 consolidated these operations to prevent a seam for the enemy to exploit. The company established a separate Operations Center to augment the battalion TOC and to provide dedicated supervision of their subordinate elements supporting security operations. The FSC would not only conduct sustainment duties of maintenance, recovery, DFAC, and fueling but would also simultaneously conduct vehicle interdiction, roof guards, entry control point, and local security patrols as part of Operation Sha'ab Shield VII, COP Callahan security zone operations (CCSZ). This enduring operation was to prevent a catastrophic attack against COP Callahan.

The brigade continued to load SIGINT targets for Hussnaiyah, causing nightly raids into the city. B/1-68 caught a brigade HVI, but the continuous raids into the city of Hussnaiyah would allow the enemy to develop the battalion's pattern of operation. Special Groups attempted to set an ambush but failed as B/1-68 engaged and destroyed the primary positions. This led into the second quarter of operations as the enemy direct fire engagements increased with open gun fights in both Sha'ab and Hussnaiyah.

B/1-68 established overwatch positions at key access points into the city. The residents bermed these access points to deny our entrance. With the enemy activity in the battalion's southern sector increasing, we moved south out of Boob-A-Sham and Fahama, and B/1-68 assumed all of Istiqlal with the primary mission of maintaining open LOC along ASR Dover. B/1-68 established tank/Bradley positions outside of Hussnaiyah and Boob-Al-Sham. Special Groups out of Hussnaiyah would conduct nightly attacks on the heavy section, only to be destroyed by direct fire from the ground forces or engaged and destroyed by Air Weapons Teams (AWT).

The violence from Special Groups increased throughout the battalion's sector beginning in Sha'ab in the vicinity of Sharoofi Mosque. The battalion conducted Operation LION FLOOD. This was a coordinated clearing operation between D/1-68, C/1-68, and the 3-4-1 National Police. It was the culmination of enemy attack in Sha'ab. Violence within Sadr City would attempt to spill south and west within our sector. We would assume additional battle space as the brigade would consolidate adjacent units.

We would establish a security zone west of Sadr City and receive an additional Stryker Company (A/1-21IN) and a Tank Company (C/1-64AR) to prevent the flow of personnel and accelerants in and out of Sadr City. D/1-68 would continue to deny the enemy within Sha'ab, and soon C/1-68 would assume combat operations within Jamilla, south of Sadr City. The battalion would again receive additional battle space along with an additional Stryker Company (C/1-27IN). The battalion would create joint operating areas. C/1-64AR and A/1-21IN secured the western boundary of Sadr City along Route Grizzlies, reinforcing key ISF checkpoints.

These units maintained 24/7 positions to deny the enemy freedom to maneuver in and out of Sadr City. C/1-68AR and C/1-27IN operated out of COP Ford and conducted created a joint operating area within the southern community of Jamilla. C/1-27IN would occupy two patrol bases within Jamilla, Patrol Base Florida and Patrol Base Texas. These patrol bases were to allow coalition forces the ability to maneuver within Jamilla and prevent the enemy from emplacing IEDs. This would allow the brigade to provide support to additional units and contain additional violence from spilling out of Sadr City. This was the start of OPERATION LION FIRESTORM.

Combat operations in the vicinity continued after the continued presence at PBs Texas and Florida. C/1-68 conducted mounted armored patrols in three vehicle sections combining M1A2 Abrams and M2 ODS Bradleys to create very lethal hunter/killer teams. The next phase would be to seize an abandoned IP station (Thawra II) at the intersection of Routes Delta and Gold. The battalion developed a concept to protect route clearance assets to reach enemy defensive emplacements. Combined arms route clearance team (CARCT) consisted of the standard route clearance element but would be augmented by EOD teams and the new hunter/killer team to provide overwatch.

This would provide security and allow route clearance to identify enemy munitions and sequentially allow EOD to reduce the hazards. The route to Thawra II was cleared to Route Gold, allowing ISF to occupy and hold the IP station. Once the ISF had occupied positions within Jamilla, the battalion was ordered to prepare defensive obstacles along Route Gold to prevent the enemy from moving along major lines of communication. The battalion would block Routes Bama, Cali, Texas, and Zona using CARCT during periods of darkness. D&C/1-68 would provide security and emplace concrete barriers, while C/1-27IN would establish strong points and overwatch operations.

Enemy contact would be heavy with the unit's tanks and Bradleys taking multiple strikes from EFPs. Company mechanics and F/1-68 would repair vehicles struck by EFPs and have them back in the fight within 24 hours. The next phase would be to separate Sadr City from the Jamilla Market and prevent further financial support. To accomplish this, the battalion in conjunction with adjacent units would construct a concrete wall separating the two communities. C&D/1-68 would conduct nightly CARCT operations and then emplace concrete barriers during periods of darkness.

The brigade directed the battalions to conduct separate operations simultaneously during these periods. This would allow the enemy to reseed engagement areas with EFPs, and prior to emplacing barriers, the battalion would require route clearance to clear lanes for emplacement. The battalions began cooperating and conducted continuous operations along Route Gold. C/1-68 was the main effort conducting CARCT, securing support elements and emplacing barriers. D/1-68 would provide route security and also overwatch the brigade's support areas. Within 30 days, the GOLD WALL was constructed from Route Aeros to Route Grizzlies along Route Gold. During the 30 days of barrier emplacement, the enemy would launch attack after attack with no avail. The Silver Lions did not lose one soldier and only received minor combat injuries, medevac'ing less than a dozen soldiers.

The third quarter of operations began with the ISF occupying key checkpoints within Sadr City. As part of the GOI agreement with Sadrist, coalition forces would not occupy Sadr City but would be prepared to reinforce the ISF. The brigade would readjust boundaries again, leaving the battalion with all of Hay Ur. We would lose all of the attachments but receive A/1-68AR from FOB Prosperity. The company was conducting escort duty and ECP operations in the Green Zone. They would be assigned to occupy JSS-Ur. At this point, we had operational control of three JSSs (Istiqlal, Sha'ab, and Ur), COP Ford, and FOB Callahan.

As the unit returned to a steady state of operations, the improvised rocket assisted mortar (IRAM) threat increased. With the attack on JSS-Sadr City, FOB Callahan was the next target. The enemy was unable to successfully target FOB Callahan. This reinvigorated security zone operations around all JSSs, COPs and FOBs. A tank section was placed on Route Sharps to deny the enemy from historic launch sites. Also, vehicle interdiction and security disruption patrols went to continuous operations. F/1-68AR was augmented with sections from C, D, and E/1-68A. JSS-Ur was attacked but received no casualties and only minor injuries. Also, the brigade would lose the 1/2 SCR, and this would cause a shift in boundaries and battle space. The battalion would lose all of Istiqlal to 2-25 BCT (with a joint operating area within Saba Quasar), and Hay Ur to 1-6IN along with C/1-68AR. The battalion would gain Adamiyah and a battery (A Battery, 3-29 FA) from the Green Zone.

As the third quarter would end, our battle space included the tactical control of JSS Suleik, Adamiyah, Sha'ab COP Apache, and FOB Callahan. The focus of most of the third quarter and beginning of the fourth quarter was to invigorate economic growth by distributing micro-grants to businesses that had been disrupted by combat operations. The battalion focused on bringing normalcy to the Iraqi people through targeting second- and third-tier criminals, partnering with ISF, transitioning the Sons of Iraq security forces to ISF and work programs, and removing accelerants through aggressive cache sea

After Action Report

Memoirs
#SADRCITYBOYS

The following series of essays are literary contributions by #SadrCityBoys. These articles are personal memoirs. While the authors have given special permission for these essays to be reprinted here, each article belongs to the author and who each hold the normal ownership rights that every copyright owner enjoys.

SGT BOONE
CUTLER

SWET
(Sewage, Water, Electricity, and Trash)

Reprinted with Permission from
CallSign Voodoo
by *Boone Cutler*

*Would you put your trash in the dumpster
or leave it for the goats if you thought
you might get killed over it?*

American forces established several public services projects to help improve the living conditions and quality of life for the people of Sadr City. We implemented programs to solve problems with their sewage, water, electricity, and trash disposal (SWET). A tremendous amount of energy and resources were dedicated to this effort to make the living conditions in Sadr City more livable, but Jaysh al-Mahdi influences every action in Sadr City even when it comes to the people helping themselves. Jaysh al-Mahdi told the people that if they helped

233

the "occupiers" do anything; they would be considered traitors of Islam and be hurt or killed.

In the movie Apocalypse Now the lead character, played by Martin Sheen, meets up with Col. Kurtz, played by Marlon Brando, and Brando recites his famous horror monologue. In that monologue, he describes how he saw a pile of inoculated arms that were cut off children because they accepted help from the Americans. The same mentality existed in Sadr City. So the SWET projects received little or no support from the people. Surviving day-to-day and being free from Jaysh al-Mahdi coercion meant that the people were going to have to live in sewage-filled streets, and they piled their trash in the roads instead of participating in the trash collection program.

Americans established programs that simply required basic participation in order for them to work. The system was not much different than apartment living in the United States, Germany, or anyplace else. Central collection points were built where it could be picked up weekly, but the people couldn't be seen trying to help themselves. So trash would get piled six to ten feet high outside of the receptacles approximately fifteen away where it would have to be picked up with shovels by the trash truck drivers. They would rather leave it for the goats to pick through with no regard for the barefoot kids. Jaysh al-Mahdi ensured the projects would fail, and that gave them something else for which they could publicly blame the Americans.

Would you put your trash in the dumpster or leave it for the goats if you thought you might get killed over it? Everybody was in on the game, and there wasn't much more that we could do. It was more than a little frustrating to see children playing alongside sewage running down the street for absolutely no reason. The trash clogged the drainage systems, so the area became flooded with sewage. The sewage contaminated the drinking water, and people got sick. This was a recurring issue and all because of the fucking trash problem that would never be resolved because Jaysh al-Mahdi forced people to dump it in the street. It wasn't like people were being beaten to death over the issue. It was nothing overt. It was simply understood, and they didn't question it.

When Iraqi contractors were hired to repair and to build the sewage system, Jaysh al-Mahdi exploited that opportunity and extorted money from the contractors to make sure the work was never completed. I have heard of multi-million-dollar contracts being picked to the bone. Each contractor hired a subcontractor, and Jaysh al-Mahdi took a portion of the money from the contractor and each subcontractor until there was simply not enough money to do the work.

Trash trucks were purchased and set up on routes to pick up the trash from receptacles and designated trash collection points, but when the people were forced not to use the collection points, the receptacles did little good to help solve the problem. They piled trash around the receptacles but not in them. I think that it meant that they wanted to use them but couldn't. These people tried to do good. The people knew and understood the cause of the problem and were willing to help themselves, but they weren't permitted to assist Americans in any way. The drivers of the trash trucks were also not permitted to do their job.

Clean drinking water in the heat of summer was a problem. One time during a patrol, we went into a sector to investigate a point of origin for a mortar attack against our FOB. What we found were people who hadn't received water for five days. Five days anywhere is a long time to go without water, but in the heat of the Iraqi summer where the temperature reaches 130 degrees it's deadly. I asked the people what happened to the water delivery, and they told me that the delivery drivers wouldn't fill the water tanks unless the drivers were bribed. The water program was provided for free to the people of Sadr City from the government, and there was plenty of water. But the drivers were collecting bribes from the poor people of Sadr City and giving it to the Sadr Bureau.

Everything they needed was given to them, and they either couldn't take advantage of it or they had to pay illegal bribes to receive it. Jaysh al-Mahdi was behind the extortion of the contractors, and they even extorted the people for water. Very rarely would people step forward to acknowledge the root of the problem, but on occasion they did, and the problem was always Jaysh al-Mahdi.

There were District Advisory Councils set up to represent the people. On the day we found the people of the sector who had gone without water for five days, we went to the DAC to find out its version of the problem. The DAC representative stated that the driver couldn't deliver to that sector because it wasn't safe for him to stop. The DAC lied about the situation, and within ten minutes a DAC representative was on the phone with someone from the water station. Thirty minutes later, a truck had safely arrived without a problem and delivered the water. We were fighting the effects of Jaysh al-Mahdi on all fronts. The people of that sector were sick, and their children were even lethargic, but still nothing was done to help them until we came along.

When we initially went to the sector and discovered the problem, I asked if anyone had gone to the DAC to tell them of the problem. As TPT, we always tried to educate the people by telling them that they had rights and they had a representative who could help. Repeatedly, the people told us that the DAC only took care of itself. The truth was more that the DAC was infiltrate and controlled by Jaysh al-Mahdi. We told the people to organize themselves, drive to the DAC to complain together, and make their representatives work for them. On that day, we went and did it for them, but several citizens also went to the DAC.

When we returned to the sector, we were met by the citizens who did organize like we told them to do. They were still holding their filled-out complaint forms in their hands. When they went to the DAC, they were told to leave at gunpoint and the DAC refused to hear their complaints. Their concerns went unheard, and if American soldiers hadn't solved the problem for them then nothing would have gotten accomplished. The DAC is supposed to represent the people, but they didn't because they were, also, afraid they would be killed.

One night on patrol we stopped because shots were fired as we drove by. The patrol turned around and found that a local DAC member had been kidnapped while driving through the city with his wife and young son. Jaysh al-Mahdi abducted the DAC member. His tortured, lifeless body was found the next day. We missed the abduction by no more than three minutes, and it happened just after we drove by. I held that man's son, who was inconsolable, as the DAC member's wife wept hysterically. There was nothing we could do for them. Oddly enough, there were Iraqi Police in trucks within view who heard and saw nothing. They didn't even respond to the shots being fired.

We told an Iraqi Police Officer to put out a broadcast of the vehicle descriptions we got from the scene. Later, we went to the Iraqi Police Station, and they told us that no broadcast was put out and that they didn't even know about the abduction. Jaysh al-Mahdi controls the DAC and the IPs in Sadr City. Anyone who steps out of line or opposes them is served the same fate. They can be kidnapped, tortured, or killed whenever the Punishment Committee gets the order from Muqtada, and they do it without consequence.

Going to the DAC on the day of the water shortage was only a band aid solution, and it's most likely that we only stopped the problem for a short time. For the long term we hoped to have affected one person who might be willing to stand up and resist them: maybe a mother who had a sick child because of the induced water shortage or maybe a child who can see that Jaysh al-Mahdi creates problems and that the Americans were there to help. Maybe a child of a slain DAC member could be the new leader of Iraq and oppose the Punishment Committee.

As a TPT, we do what we can to influence as many people as possible to expose darkness and be willing to set themselves free. On the day we returned to that water-deprived sector, we used our loudspeaker and gave a script to a local elder to read. From his mouth, the people heard a message. They heard him say that the people were victorious and that they weren't willing to pay illegal bribes for a gift that was given to them by their legitimate Iraqi government. The people cheered, and our TPT used the conditions to empower them. That was a good day for Tactical PsyOp and a great day for the people in one sector of Sadr City.

1SGT GREG
L. BAKER

NO ONE
EVER HURT US
WITHOUT PAYBACK
by Greg L. Baker

March 25, 2008 was my 44th birthday, and I was 4 months into a 15-month deployment in the Abu Ghraib district of Iraq as a Platoon Sergeant in C Co 2-21 Infantry out of Schofield Barracks, HI. Early that morning, I received word that I was to leave my platoon and report to A Co at Camp Victory to assume duties as their First Sergeant.

I hitched a ride with our 3rd Platoon and arrived at A Co HQ around mid-day. Almost immediately, CPT Scott Bailey greeted me.

"Hey, First Sergeant, we just got word we're deploying to Sadr City in a few hours. Are you coming?"

Of course, my answer was something along the lines of "Hell, yeah." A few hours later, we'd completed our preparations and were, indeed, rolling into eastern Baghdad.

We reached JSS Ur, a bus depot on the northwest side of

Sadr City, in the early hours of March 26, 2008. By 1700, we were in our first of many daily gunfights. After two weeks of fighting the Jaish al Madhi in the streets with everything from rifles to M1 tanks and F16s, we thought we had a pretty good idea of where and how to interdict their teams that emplaced the explosively formed penetrators (EFPs) that killed and wounded so many American and Iraqi soldiers. CPT Scott Bailey's plan was a plain simple "old school" platoon-area ambush. On the night of April 11, 2008, several squad-sized elements infiltrated from JSS Ur on foot to separate ambush positions with our sniper team, Gator Eye, and mortar section on one flank as a security element.

Just after daylight, Doc McMillan spotted insurgents attempting to emplace the bomb. Doc, SFC Jean Morris, SGT Bob Barthel, and SGT Nate Rolens engaged and killed two of them with M4s, and PFC Ringo Whigham killed a third with his SAW. After assaulting and clearing the objective, Doc treated one, but he died anyway. The team captured a motorcycle and a van used by the bad guys.

Jaish al Madhi was a well-organized force, and they began to assemble a quick reaction force (QRF) to attack SFC Morris's element. Within minutes of the ambush, well over a dozen bad guys armed with AKs, machine-guns, and RPGs gathered in front of a house to receive orders and prepare their attack. Unfortunately for them, their assembly area was less than 100 meters from the position occupied by Gator Eye and the mortar team.

SGT Storm Litzler and SPC Michael Esposito engaged with precision fire from their suppressed M110 and M24 sniper systems, rapidly killing at least 12 before coming under RPG and PKM fire. They called for our QRF for extraction and fought a running fight to the linkup point with the platoon from B Co. SFC James

Dean and SSG Charlie McNeely managed to get them out safely while killing several more insurgents who fired from rooftops.

The 4th ID Commanding General, MG Jeffrey Hammond, drove out in a HMMWV the next day from Camp Victory and pinned Bronze Stars on twelve of our guys right in front of our luxurious blue portajohn.

The operation likely killed the insurgets who detonated an EFP against a convoy coming to resupply us on March 30, 2008 killing SGT Terrell Gilmore of the Louisiana National Guard. No one ever hurt us without payback.

Storm got shot on our last op together on April 26, 2008 and was medevaced to Qatar (Thanks, Chris Greca, for the EVAC). He didn't stay gone long. It was only a couple of weeks before I got a call to come pick him up at Camp Liberty. I'm pretty sure he went AWOL from the hospital to get back to us.

Doc McMillan was killed less than three months later on July 8, 2008 near Nasr wa Salaam.

CPT LOGAN
VEATH

244

THE
WORST DAY

by Logan Veath

There are a few things beyond your control, which will haunt you throughout your life. You will spend countless hours and exorbitant amounts of energy replaying the events which led up to that moment, the moment itself, and the chaotic aftermath. You will play devil's advocate, think about the shouldas, couldas, and wouldas. It's a vicious circle that never ends until you are able to make peace in your mind and soul. Though you recognize the result was not what you wanted, you can know that you could not have done anything more to change it. Sometimes this isn't even enough.

SGT John Kyle Daggett an all-American type of male. He was an only son and brother. He was Jack's, his father's, pride and joy. They would spend their time outdoors, fishing, hunting, and enjoying each other's company. He was everything Jack wanted in a son. To Colleen, his mother, he was the handsome, honest, and *tough young man who was raised right. He was one of the good ones. The kind of man that dads pray their daughters will meet and end up marrying. Kyle was one of those men you could trust to get things done the right way. He had a zest for life, particularly when times were stressful, chaotic, and dark. He was one of those Soldiers that you hoped others would emulate. A commander would wish for a dozen SGT John Kyle Daggetts.*

★★★

For the majority of the men of Bravo Company (Bushmasters), 1-14th INF Regt, May 1st, 2008 was the worst day of their arduous fifteen month deployment to Iraq. The events of that day have caused many Bushmaster Soldiers to find ways to medicate themselves to numb the pain. It haunts them because they feel responsible. There is a misguided belief that the situation would have been different had they done even one small thing differently. There is the wish that the outcome would have been different; that 15 years later while reminiscing around a campfire, you could say, "That was a close one." Then you would look your brother in the eye and silently communicate how grateful you are that he is sitting with you and sharing the moment.

Six months before the deployment, the Bushmaster Company Commander told his company of 178 Infantrymen that they would go into Iraq, honorably complete their mission, and return home safely to their loved ones.

He had deployed multiple times before which included participating in the invasions of Afghanistan and Iraq He had taken many young men to war and brought all of them home before. Each time he went, he did the same thing. He did his best to instill confidence and courage into his men. He believed form followed consciousness. By confidently stating it, it would be so. He told them that he would bring them all home alive. It was a promise that he had made to others and kept. Maybe it was over-confidence, ego, or an overwhelming desire to be their leader. Nevertheless, it was a promise over which he had no control.

During those six months, these men transformed from a light infantry company to a Stryker infantry company. Learning new tactics, ways of fighting, and field training exercises to prepare them for combat took countless hours away from their families. The emotional toll it took on the Soldiers and their families was great. The men knew they needed to train and prepare for war because it was one of the best ways to return to their loved ones. At the same time, they sacrificed those finite and precious moments with their families by missing birthdays, anniversaries, and once-in-a-lifetime moments like births and birthdays. It tore them up inside knowing they would be missing so many things over the next 21 months. But they were Warriors and brothers, so the Bushmasters committed themselves to each other and to their craft.

At the same time, Muqtada al Sadr, the sinister Shia cleric and leader of the Mahdi militia in Sadr City, had decided that the new Iraqi government was not religious enough for him or his Shia brethren. As a result, he began doing what he could to disrupt and destroy the stability of the Iraqi government and prevent them from having any Western-influenced freedoms. He and his militia spent the same 6 months that the Bushmasters had spent transforming from a light infantry company to a Stryker infantry company, focusing on the production and distribution of thousands of improvised explosive devices (IEDs), hidden in curbs and sidewalks throughout Sadr City, ready to destroy whatever was within 100 feet when detonated. Much of Muqtada's bomb-making supplies came from Iran.

Named after Muqtada al-Sadr's father (Mohammed Sadeq al-Sadr) who was murdered by Saddam Hussein, Sadr City is a densely populated slum in the northeast corner of Baghdad. At the time that Bravo Company was deployed to Iraq in 2008, it densely housed approximately one million people 5 square miles. It was a housing project that Saddam Hussein (a Sunni) neglected due to his discrimination against its heavy Shia population.

Concurrent with these clandestine and lethal activities, Muqtada also created a sanctuary within Sadr City by working with the Prime Minister and Allied Forces. This brokered deal prevented any American forces from moving North of "Al Quds Street" also known as Phase Line

"Gold" into the inner parts of Sadr City. In essence, this gave the militia the ability to recon, prepare, engage US forces, and return to an area that the US forces would not be able to enter.

After booby-trapping and preparing much of the city, he had his Mahdi Army begin firing rockets into the International Zone (Green Zone) in central Baghdad where the Iraqi government and supporting groups from all over the world were working to create the necessary infrastructure for the country to function. Many people were injured, maimed, or killed due to these rockets.

In late March 2008, the progress of the Allied Forces was starting to grind to a halt. LTG Austin and MG Hammonds, however, would not allow that to happen. They wanted to ensure that progress would continue by placing an emphasis on using American forces to coordinate operations, but put the nascent Iraqi Army in the lead. Further, they wanted to destroy Muqtada al Sadr and his Mahdi Army by eradicating their ability to destabilize the fragile infrastructure.

All of the units in Sadr City were stretched thin with all of the different counter insurgency operations (providing food, water, security, creating infrastructure) and combat operations (raids, ambushes, etc.) It was frustrating to have so many tasks and just enough Soldiers to barely accomplish them. Muqtada decided this was the perfect time to begin open aggressive attacks. When the rocket attacks began, the American forces needed reinforcements to provide superior firepower and reduce the enemy's ability to continue their attacks. There was a need for more American forces to quell the attacks.

At the same time, the Bushmasters were creating a tactical outpost in the Sal-a-din province of Iraq, which was located in the most northern region of the 2nd Stryker Brigade Combat Team's zone— nearly 60 miles away from Sadr City. They had spent the previous month patrolling the sparse rural area and building a combat outpost. The Bushmasters were internally struggling with what a modern warrior was. Many of them had signed the dotted line because they wanted to close with and destroy the enemy. They wanted to test their mettle in combat. They had a thirst to know what they were when the bullets started to land close. They had completed one raid in which no shots were fired. They spent long hot days trudging through small villages of mud huts, talking with the local Iraqi citizens, searching for weapons caches, and providing resources for these villages to build infrastructure. It wasn't what the young Warriors expected.

Then the call came, at 2100 hours 28 March 2008, the message belted over the radio for the Bushmasters to bring their three platoons to battalion headquarters and be ready to move to Sadr City. There was a sudden energy in the air. The men knew deep down they were going to do exactly what they signed up to do. The Brigade had taken the hammer to the 'In case of Emergency, break glass' and the Bushmasters were released. There was pride and elation that we were chosen for this dangerous mission. There was a nervousness, the type of nervousness people feel when they are about to compete. The butterflies in their stomachs continued to grow because they knew it wasn't a game. This would be life and death. The Bushmasters were called to the tip of the spear, to face an enemy intent on killing them. It was time to be the Warriors they knew and trained to be.

By 0100 hours, the Bushmasters were headed to Baghdad and the headquarters of 1-2 SCR where they would be operationally attached. They then rolled into headquarters and received the mission to prevent rockets from being fired into the Green Zone by denying the insurgents launch sites. By 0600 that morning, they were in the battlespace. Despite not sleeping for more than 24 hours, the Bushmasters moved to their positions with a sense of purpose. For the next 3-4 days, much of the company leadership slept for less than ten total hours. In those first days, there was a constant and steady fight between the insurgents and American forces. This required the Leaders to monitor the battle, predict what the enemy would do next, and rotate the three platoons to ensure they slept, ate, and had the energy to fight when the battle intensified. By all accounts, the Bushmasters were the epitome of Warriors. There was a beauty in the way they operated and took care of one another. It became obvious that these men loved one another and would do everything they could to protect each other.

For the next month, the Bushmasters fought a constant battle against the Mahdi Army— fighting the insurgents day and night. During that time, they did not have hot food, warm showers, toilets, or beds to sleep. Sleep came to them in four-to-six-hour increments or whenever they could catch a quick nap. Several of the Bushmasters had been wounded from IEDs and countless engagements with the insurgents. They were surviving and it seemed as though nothing could kill them. They weren't so brazen to not follow their training or make stupid decision to tempt fate. However, by aggressive action, it seemed things worked out in their favor.

Additionally, these young men did everything they could to protect the innocent civilians who were caught in the middle of both armies by providing them medical and dental triage as well as food for their starving families. And all of this while putting the Iraqi Army in the lead per Petraeus's intent. The American forces would push the Iraqi Army to conduct raids, interact with the local populace, and be placed at the tip of the spear with the American Forces. It felt like a lion teaching its cubs how to hunt and kill by facilitating and providing them with easy missions to gain their confidence. If there was something that went wrong or the Iraqi Army couldn't or wouldn't handle, the Bushmasters would step in and crush it.

The Iraqi Army had proven time and again that it was incapable of standing toe-to-toe against the insurgents.

The Company Commander begged and pleaded for them to stay in position and not retreat, but they didn't listen. It was like dealing with someone who talks a good game, and when it comes time to walk the talk they find excuses. It was a defeatist approach. Always there was a reason, the Company Commander had to nimbly counter their arguments and prove it was a lack of desire. Putting them in the lead was also difficult because the Bushmasters wanted to lead by example. In doing so, the Iraqi Army was more than willing to let the Bushmasters do their job for them. The majority of the time, however, the Iraqi Army would stay. But it was not uncommon for them to retreat or slink away because they were afraid. The assumption was the majority of the young Soldiers wanted to be like us. However, their leadership was based on the old Iraqi Army standards of, Do as I say and not as I do. Much of the leadership was based on fear. There were some good young leaders and a few older ones which had courage and the intestinal fortitude to do the hard right. However, a few bad apples could spoil the whole lot. When dealing with these bad apples, there was a certain revulsion the Bushmasters felt. It was difficult to deal with cowards. It was the antithesis of what a warrior was and what the Bushmasters believed in.

Frustration was building within the Bushmaster ranks. They had quelled the violence, destroyed and captured insurgents, and stabilized the area but felt like they had to force the Iraqi Army and Police to take the lead. In short, it was a practice in futility because you can't make someone who didn't want to do their job, do their job. Some of the Iraqis were from Sadr City. It wasn't uncommon in Iraq for the insurgents to make examples of their families. If the insurgents could identify or suspect another Iraqi was working against them or helping the Americans, they would kill, torture, rape that Iraqi's family. Many of them wanted to wear masks to prevent being identified. Some of their leaders were lazy and wanted all of the glory but didn't want to do what was necessary to properly ascertain the glory. This was foreign to the Bushmasters. It was very difficult to understand and much harder to accept. However, training had taught them to put those feelings aside and do what was needed and right.

This problem became apparent when the Iraqi Police force abandoned a police headquarters, the closest secured location to the insurgents' sanctuary. The police compound was surrounded by a fifteen-foot-tall wall with guard towers at the corners and centers of two walls. Inside the compound was a small five-room clinic, covered parking area, a couple of small outbuildings, and the headquarters building. The headquarters building was maybe two stories tall. But directly across Phase Line Gold were several buildings that were three, four, even seven stories tall. The Iraqi police had left their uniforms, weapons, and gear strewn throughout the building. It was in complete disarray and no way of accounting for what was missing. However, we knew that civilians and insurgents had already started looting the station by the time we got there.

General Hammond, the Division Commander, would not accept this. General Hammond was an aviator who had played quarterback (ahead of Brett Farve) at University of Southern Mississippi. As many of us know, it takes a little bit of ego to play quarterback. His reputation throughout the Army was that he was extremely confident and made his staff do what he wanted. It may be his football career or how he saw the world, but he equated everything to football. It worked for the most part and provided an analogy most people could understand. When he latched on to a carefully planned idea, particularly if it was his idea, it was rare for him to deviate. He loved the Soldiers and felt most shortcomings of Soldiers of any unit was due to leadership. Hell hath no fury, if MG Hammond saw an officer not leading by example or doing the right thing. He ordered American forces to occupy this compound to prevent insurgents and civilians from looting and taking possession from it. He called it a patrol base and wanted them to secure this location 24/7.

But the problem was that 1-2 SCR was already spread very thin with all of the tasks assigned to it. The only way to achieve the mission ordered by the Division Commander was to occupy the compound during daylight hours and then leave under the cover of darkness to complete other tasks and missions.

The compound was surrounded by much taller buildings where anyone who wanted to find out what was going on behind the walls of the compound could simply climb the stairs to one of the top floors. From the time the Bushmasters occupied the compound, they received direct and indirect fire from the Sadr City sanctuary. After two to three days, the Iraqi Army brought a company of soldiers to occupy the police headquarters. General Hammond decided American forces would stand shoulder-to-shoulder with their Iraqi counterparts and continue to use the compound as a patrol base.

When the Bushmasters occupied the compound, it became evident that the Iraqi Army was undisciplined. Within the first twenty-four hours, there was trash all over the place, leftover food left out, and various other items strewn throughout the building. The Iraqi soldiers had placed beds and cots all over the place, and many of them were partially dressed and lounging around. There was an abundance of tasks to be done in the compound which ranged from picking up trash from the looting, pulling security, and rearranging and returning equipment to storage rooms. It appeared that the Iraqi Army had disdain for rudimentary soldiering tasks which, of course, is the foundation for everything else. The Bushmasters were appalled at the behavior and indifference these Iraqis were displaying. Much of this was due to their leadership or lack of. A lot of young Iraqis wanted to be like the American forces. They dressed and made their equipment look like American forces. They were proud to show and relate to us. It is like when a son tries to dress in his dad's clothes. It seems more and more they lacked solid leadership. Those individual Iraqi soldiers were coached and mentored by American Soldiers. The Bushmasters were able to help some of the young Iraqi Squad Leaders start getting their soldiers to do the right things. Those soldiers were thrown into a basic training course and into combat in a condensed timeframe. It was difficult for the American forces to empathize with the situation, partly due to knowing the type of behavior the Iraqis displayed would lead to bad results. These would include losing Soldiers, harming the civilian population, and general disorder.

Another problem was that this Iraqi Army seemed to lack intestinal fortitude and heart, particularly by the higher ranking. There was a general level of apathy present within the Iraqi Army, and there were several instances during our time in Sadr City when the Iraqi Army demonstrated that we could not depend upon them. A prime example was when they were in a firefight and decided to have lunch instead of closing with and destroying the enemy. They wanted to retreat from their fighting positions several times and, for the most part, the Bushmasters had to coax them to stay in place. The Bushmasters knew that the Iraqi soldiers wanted to be like them, but they did not want to put in the hard work to get there. It was extremely frustrating for the Bushmasters to watch a group of people who neither could nor would help themselves, particularly when there were difficulties.

From the time the Bushmasters began occupying the police station, several mortar rounds landed in the compound along with sporadic gunfire and the occasional single shot (possibly a "sniper"). It was obvious that the enemy knew they were occupying the police station. As each day passed, the rounds were getting closer to their positions. The Company Commander, First Sergeant, Platoon Leaders, and Platoon Sergeants knew that this was a tactically unsound mission because the patrol base violated all of the tactical rules for a patrol base.

The Soldiers knew that it violated these common-sense rules. Like good US Infantrymen, they continued the mission. The company leadership had a meeting to discuss this mission, and they determined there were other viable courses of action which would meet the mission and have the same outcomes. Also, the company would continue to occupy the patrol base and make the Iraqi Army do their jobs.

The Company Commander felt deeply in his bones that this mission would end up with his Soldiers wounded or—God forbid—dead. Without telling the company leadership, he took the Squadron Commander aside and discussed the unsound mission, providing his own logic.

The Squadron Commander knew and understood exactly what the Company Commander was telling him and had already voiced his opinion to the chain of command. The Squadron Commander cracked a smile and chuckled a little with the Company Commander. In his fatherly way, he explained to him the patrol base mission was the idea of General Hammond. The Company Commander, like MG Hammond, believed this to be a tactical mistake and thought that he could change the General's mind. The Squadron Commander directed the Company Commander that, if he felt strongly about this mission, he should take it up the chain of command, just like he had. The Company Commander reassured him that his company would continue to execute the mission to the best of their abilities and that he would take it up the chain of command.

Later that day, the Company Commander met with the Brigade Commander who was checking the battle lines and observing what was actually happening on the ground. The Company Commander repeated the same message to the Brigade Commander. The Brigade Commander appreciated the thoughtfulness and understanding of the tactics. However, it had been discussed with higher authorities. He told the Company Commander to take it up the chain of command if he felt this strongly. It might create a change but most likely wouldn't. Within 24-48 hours, the Company Commander had met with each of the Deputy Division Commanders during their review of the battlefield and observations. They agreed with the Company Commander that tactically it was not sound. However, we needed the Iraqi Army to control this area and show the world the Iraqi Army could maintain control of a very volatile situation. Both Generals directed him to the Division Commander because this operation was his baby.

When May 1, 2008 came, 1st Platoon was occupying the police compound with the Iraqi Army. They had the Iraqi Army pulling security and managing the chaos within the compound, while the platoon sent a section (two vehicles with squads) to the intersection of Phase Line Gold and Route Alpha outside the police compound. There was intelligence supporting concern that a vehicle-borne improvised explosive device (VBIED) attack might occur.

In the late afternoon, General Hammond and his entourage moved into the company's battlespace because he wanted to check on the patrol base and ensure that the Iraqi Army was doing their part. The Company Commander met MG Hammond and escorted him throughout the compound, voicing the message of tactically unsound and alternate locations. He wanted to change things up: new location, etc. MG Hammond gave the Company Commander's comments consideration. He explained to the Company Commander there weren't many options. This patrol base was a key strategic piece of terrain and had strategic ramifications if we failed. They both understood the Iraqi Army had to maintain control or else lose the momentum and halt the progress the Iraqis had made.

Finally, the Company Commander expressed to the General that it was only a matter of time before something bad happened to his men. He told the General that, while his company was stalwart in completing the mission, he wanted to know the reasoning behind the decision so that he could inform them. The General told the Company Commander that he was correct that the plan violated the tactical rules. However, at the strategic level it was required, and that was more important. Basically, he wanted the company to show the whole world that the American Forces would stand shoulder to shoulder with the Iraqi Army, and he wanted this message to be known by the Mahdi Army and all insurgents.

It was a bitter pill to swallow for the Company Commander. On one hand he understood the strategic mission and the ramifications for failing. However, he knew without a doubt his men were exposed in a dangerous position. It wasn't like in the early stages of this battle, where they were able to act with violence of action and overwhelm the enemy. They were static and reactionary. His forces were proactive to a point but even then they were put in a position to react to enemy contact. This was the situation he feared. Despite actively scanning buildings in the sanctuary, it was would only be by luck to catch the enemy before they fired upon them.

After approximately thirty minutes on the ground, the Commanding General and his entourage left the compound with the Company Commander's vehicles in tow.

It might have been about two minutes after they left when there was a loud BOOM! The Company Commander could identify by the sound alone that it had come from the police compound. A sickening feeling of dread burst into his heart. He knew in his soul that something bad had happened to his men.

As he sent out the message for a situational report (SITREP) and for his entourage to turn around, his vehicles were already turning around to head back to the compound at full speed.

Suddenly, the dreaded message came over the company net.

"We have a KIA and wounded."

The Commander's heart broke. A myriad of thoughts poured through his mind.

Who was it? Who was wounded? Where was the enemy? What could he do to influence the fight? God dammit! This was exactly what I was expressing to the General! Please, don't be dead. Dear God, please let this report be wrong.

However, the heaviness of dread clung to him and began pulling him down. In that moment, the frustrations, malcontent, and anger of the entire company erupted. 1st Platoon unleashed the fifty caliber machine guns. The Soldiers began engaging enemy targets. The volume of firepower grew and grew. The barking of the gunfire was the Soldiers way of yelling, screaming and releasing the emotions that had been simmering. They maintained their discipline and their training kicked in identifying positions and destroying them.

The Company Commander's vehicles raced into the fight, joining 1st Platoon's vehicles and bringing with them the immense firepower a Stryker could bring to the fight. A section of 1st Platoon Soldiers who bore the wounded took off. The radio crackled again.

"We are headed down Route Cobra, headed to the field hospital."

The Company Commander's men began identifying buildings where they were receiving enemy fire, their fifty caliber machine guns bursting with 6-9 round bursts. A soldier launched a shoulder fired rocket at an enemy position and hit its target.

For the Company Commander, his rage was cold and calculated. Things slowed down. He began grabbing and using all assets available to him. His company was able to identify three to four buildings from which they were receiving fire. He used close air support and every authorized weapon system. He guided the deployment of three 500lb JDAMS (bombs) on enemy occupied buildings, even those that were "danger close", leveling them. As the smell of gunpowder, smoke, and diesel fuel filled their noses and after their ears were ringing from firepower, they watched as the close air support cannons fired on enemy positions, destroying the identified buildings. There was an elegance to the precision of these weapon systems. They watched as the rounds hit the buildings, heard the impact and sounds of them firing from the close air support. They wanted to make sure that any and everyone associated with that ambush was dead. There would be no doubt in their enemy's mind that they would lay waste to all enemy positions when attacked. We were precise enough to locate and destroy the enemy.

The feeling and actions were a double edged sword. On one side there is the release and the ability to inflict the necessary harm upon those trying to kill you. On the other side, there has to be an awareness to ensure you are not harming the civilians and bystanders caught in the middle. This rage is not pretty nor should it be a sense of pride. It is one of the ugliest things you can become. There is a shame which comes from seeing this dangerous and horrible side of yourself. As a human being, you try to be a good human being. There is a sanctity of life that you hold dear. Most of us in our wildest dreams would not believe we have this rage in us. If or when it comes out, it cuts you to the core. The shame and disgust you have for yourself knowing you have this in you, stays with you for a long time. It is hard to discuss with people because it makes you feel like a monster. As a warrior, you are the one who fights those monsters.

As the fight wound down, more thoughts cascaded through the collective mind of the company.

How could this happen to us? Why was it that Ranger Daggett was killed? What are we doing here? We are here to help these people from years of oppression, yet all we seem to do is babysit grown adults who don't want to fight for their basic freedoms. We consistently have to put "boots to ass" to get them to do their jobs. We care more for their basic freedoms than they do. Why do we continue to help these people when they won't help themselves? If they weren't such cowards, we wouldn't be sitting here pulling security and waiting for the enemy to hit us. Why can't we move into the sanctuary and take away the enemy's ability to fight? How do you destroy the Mahdi Army when you can't get to them?

These thoughts were interrupted by radio communications from the section travelling to the field hospital. They had finally arrived and were on their way back. As silence fell on the battlefield, they pulled back from the battle, leaving the Iraqi Army to occupy the compound.

They gathered at the battalion's base parking lot. The men exited their vehicles. Most kept their kits on, and there was an energy of sorrow and gloom with them. Some of the men went off by themselves. Others gathered together. They all looked into each other's eyes but not many words were spoken. Tears and hugs were given freely. Silently, they prayed for God's divine intervention.

Please, save Ranger Daggett and the others that were wounded.

Some of the men found things to break. Others just yelled and cussed at nothing but the sky. The explosive rage quietly settled back into their hearts.

The Squadron Commander found the Company Commander standing alone, trying to set the example for his Bushmasters by holding back tears. The Squadron Commander hugged him and told him that he was so very sorry. The Company Commander shook his head and replied that he knew it was coming. He asked the Squadron Commander what was happening with the wounded and where they were being sent. The Squadron Commander told him that there were some conflicting reports, but there were no KIAs: both Soldiers were alive but badly wounded. Once they were stabilized, they would be moved to Germany and eventually back to Walter Reed.

The Company Commander latched onto the news that his Soldier hadn't died and began telling his men of the news. The hope of our Soldiers surviving eliminated much of the sorrow and gloom. However, the anger and frustration silently remained in their hearts.

After a few hours, it became clear what had occurred. 1st Platoon had two vehicles pulling security at the intersection of Phase Line Gold and Route Bravo. Daggett and Steward were in the air guard hatches while the Strykers were actively scanning the buildings. The two air guard hatches are located to the rear of the vehicle on the roof. A Mahdi militia member fired an RPG and it hit the top of the vehicle. The blast severely injured Steward, mostly in the arm and shoulder.

SGT Daggett, however, absorbed most of the blast which tore most of his face off and part of his jaw. Later, the doctors at Halifax would find some of his teeth in his lungs.

When Daggett fell to the floor of the Stryker, Platoon Sergeant grabbed the Medic, exited their vehicle, and sprinted to the struck vehicle. The Platoon Leader directed his forces as combat life-saving measures were immediately taken. The Medic felt Daggett for a pulse, but there was none. Those sectioned with Daggett and Steward began casualty evacuation. Tourniquets and wound dressing were applied to the wounded as the Soldiers and Medic in the back of the Stryker were thrown about and jostled around. SPC Bosely, the Medic, began everything he was taught to do in these situations. He would not accept that Daggett was dead, so he started CPR. Every fiber in his being forced Daggett's heart to beat and his lungs to breathe. Somehow, Daggett came back to life. A pulse, faint as it was, began.

The Stryker section drove with reckless abandon through Iraqi streets. Their sole mission was to get our wounded brothers to the MEDEVAC area where they would be transferred. Nothing would stop them from getting there, and they crushed anything and everything in their way, including cars. The Stryker section moved through the city streets making it to the MEDEVAC area. The wounded were transferred and Soldiers were inspected to ensure there weren't any unidentified wounds.

A few days after the ambush, the Company Commander was able to make a phone call. He called SGT Daggett's dad, Jack. Throughout the conversation, the Company Commander profusely apologized. His voice trembled as he told Jack that he felt responsible and wished that he could do something to change the circumstances. His quiet voice quavered as talked with Jack. He felt the dread and fear from Jack, a father who was grasping for any hope his son would live and his son's actions were significant. In the sincerest way possible, the company commander described what SGT Daggett was to the company: how this Soldier was the epitome of a Ranger and Infantryman. He was a caring leader who had been placed as a Team Leader despite his lower rank. He had been given a troubled Soldier and had patiently spent time working to square him away and make him into a good Soldier. Kyle's passion for the Army and being an Infantryman was contagious. He was living out what he dreamed of doing. He was a warrior.

The Company Commander tried to reassure Jack that his son was an excellent Soldier. The Commander could hear the devastation and grief in the father's voice. No words were capable of consoling him. His heart was breaking. There was desperation in his voice as he prayed and wished that his son would survive. The Company Commander said goodbye and began to cry. Everything in his being wanted to switch places with his Soldier. He prayed to God to let this young man survive.

Over the next ten days, the company would try to get reports while SGT Daggett was in the process of flying to Walter Reed. During the flight, his cranial pressure rose to unsafe levels, so the flight was diverted to Halifax, Nova Scotia where he was stabilized. However, the doctors were not sure that he would survive a flight to Walter Reed. The Army decided to fly his parents, sister, and fiancé to Halifax. They had nine days to lay their hands upon him, hold his hand, tenderly stroke his face, run their fingers through his hair. They prayed with all of their hearts for Kyle. Kyle's loved ones watched helplessly as his vitals weakened. They could see that he was fighting to stay alive, so they continued to pray, wept, and did everything they could to encourage him to fight and live.

On May 15, 2008, John Kyle Daggett succumbed to his wounds. The anger, frustration, and defeat seized the hearts of the Bushmasters once again. This time, there was no enemy to destroy. There was no place to expel these harsh emotions. Because the Company Commander was preparing for mid-tour leave he would be flown to Arlington to be present at SGT Daggett's funeral as well as be the best man at his brother's wedding.

It was a warm day at Arlington Cemetery. The sun was shining and there was a slight breeze. On any other day, one would say it was a beautiful day. Men from SGT Daggett's platoon and the Company Commander attended the funeral. The Company Commander entered the quiet building where SGT Daggett's friends and family were gathering and where SGT Daggett's casket was placed. For the first time, he laid his eyes on Colleen,

Kyle's mother. She saw him at the same time. He tried to remain stoic out of respect, but his heart had other ideas.

His eyes welled up with tears as he gave her a crushing hug and quietly told her how sorry he was through his sobs. She started to cry, too. He could see how hurt she was—how the devastation weighed on her. She displayed the strength of an incredible mother and was able to remain composed enough to console the Company Commander. He asked her for forgiveness, and he described to her what her son meant to him and his company. He continued to tell her how sorry he was because he felt that no number of apologies would ever be enough. She told him how much her son loved the Bushmasters, and she forgave the Company Commander, displaying the love of a mother. He excused himself and quietly made his way to Jack, Kyle's father.

As he approached Jack, he saw a brokenhearted man—a father who lost his only son, his hunting buddy: his pride and joy. Once again, the Company Commander could not remain strong. He extended his hand to Jack, a handshake that quickly turned to a hug. He expressed to Jack how utterly brokenhearted he was for allowing one of his men to lose his life. He told him how guilty he felt for failing to complete a promise. He witnessed the devastation Kyle's death had upon his family. He sobbed, the tears rolling down his face. He asked for forgiveness and voiced how sorry he was. He repeated the same things he had said time and time again about this wonderful

Soldier—the impact his son had on the Bushmasters. He was a caring and compassionate leader who did the right things. He was tenacious, tough, and courageous. Jack continued to hug the Company Commander and let him know he respected and loved him.

The Company Commander made his way to SGT Daggett. He believed he had cried enough and could pull it together until he laid eyes on the wooden casket. The dam that had held the guilt, anger, sorrow, and agony burst. There was nothing he could do to stop the cascade of emotions. Once again, his eyes filled with tears and ran down his face. He began sobbing as he put his hand on the casket. He whispered to SGT Daggett.

"I am so sorry I could not protect you. I could not prevent your death. I am sorry I failed you and the promise I made you and all of the Bushmasters. I am sorry I inflicted this pain upon your family. I wish I could do something to take this all away. SGT Daggett, I wish I could have taken your place. I would give anything to be the one in that casket. Please, forgive me for not bringing you home alive."

He tried to gather himself, but every time he thought he had it together, another wave of emotion would crash upon his heart. The rest of the introductions and condolences was a blur.

At Section 60 site 8666, graveside services were started. The Army Chaplain welcomed everyone and talked about SGT Daggett. He tried his best to personalize the service. However, that is a difficult task with the numerous funerals taking place on a daily basis. The Company Commander wished the Chaplain had personally known this Soldier.

As the Sun beat down, the silence and sorrow of the moment resonated throughout the attendees. The Chaplain finished and the Old Guard began folding the flag. The Company Commander was given the honor of presenting the flags to SGT Daggett's parents. With every ounce of his being, the Company Commander tenderly held the flag and presented it to Colleen. As she cried, the Company Commander gave her a hug and spoke quietly,

"SGT Daggett was an outstanding Soldier. He was one of the good ones. As long as I breathe, your son will never be forgotten. I am so sorry."

He came to attention slowly and ceremoniously, giving the best salute he had ever rendered.

He went back for the second flag, holding it while embodying everything SGT Daggett believed in, and gave it to Jack. The Company Commander bent down and quietly spoke to him.

"I am so sorry. I wish I could have brought your only son back. He was a great young man. As long as I breathe, Kyle will never be forgotten."

Once again, the Company Commander gave one of his best salutes to honor his Soldier. Surprisingly, he was able to hold back the tears and remain stoic.

Taps was played, and the sound of sobs could be heard.

The suddenness of the first volley of the twenty-one-gun salute ripped apart the silence, causing many of the people to jump. It rang out two more times, and then it was over.

As the Company Commander, along with SFC Arambula and SPC Strot, slowly moved out of the way, they watched Jack limp to the casket and lean on it, his shoulders heaving as he wept and said goodbye to his only son and Warrior. The Company Commander watched Colleen, Kendall, and Megan console one another. In that moment, the Company Commander witnessed what true heartbreak was. He saw the eviscerated father, mother, and loved ones who would never be the same. Their worlds were turned inside out and upside down. No amount of apologies, memorials, or time could heal these wounds. Though they would continue with life, there was and always would be an emptiness that could not ever be filled.

At that moment, the Company Commander made a sacred and silent vow that he would always be there for Daggett's family. He would do everything in his being to make sure that SGT Daggett and the rest of the Soldiers who had given the ultimate sacrifice would never be forgotten. Though the Company Commander recognized that he and the Bushmasters had done everything they could that day and that there was nothing more they could have done to change the outcome, he acknowledged that the enemy had a vote as well, which took the life of a fine man and left a family forever mourning.

The Company Commander will always feel that he failed in his mission to bring everyone home alive. He wishes there were something more he could have done. Though the wiser, he beats himself up for making a promise he could not control. He repeatedly replays the memory at the end of the graveside service in his head.

SGT Daggett, I will honor your memory and ensure that you are remembered. For I will always be your Company Commander.

I am that Company Commander,

MAJ Logan Veath, US Army (Ret.)

SSG JOSE SANCHEZ
Weapons Squad Leader
A Co 3/67 4th Infantry Div
FOB Rustamiyah, Iraq

I served with SSG Sancehz in Iraq
duirng my first tour in 2006.
He's still living. but I wanted to
dedicate this poem I wrote
for him as a living tribute.

OH, WARFATHER

The perilous danger we were in...
The pride to be led by a Ranger was the biggest win
You were the Father I never had... but needed
Your words through the years I've heeded
Everything you said was as good as gold
Proven in battle brave and bold
You moved us in silence... through the dead of night
You taught us the violence to win the fight.
We are many your WarChildren with painted faces and evil grins
Each with a purpose you slotted us in
Time has passed...but the Tribe grows larger
O, to raid once more... with MY WARFATHER!

~Poem & Tribute by FELIZ PRIETO~

SSG JARROD
L. TAYLOR

A February Raid

in the War on Terror

REPRINTED WITH PERMISSION FROM

No Shit, Here I Am

by Jarrod Taylor

It was 0100. Sleep this night had been elusive at best, coming in short segments between bumps and swerves that jostled us around in the cramped troop compartment of our twenty-ton tin can as we made our way toward the drop off point for our mission. Boys in camouflage body armor, packed like sardines leaned against one another. They moved and shifted, desperately searching for some small semblance of comfort while trying to keep their legs and asses from going to sleep. A rifle magazine jammed into the inside of a thigh here, a hand grenade pinched a hip there. In the dim glow of my squad leader commo screen, their heavy eyelids slowly closed behind the lenses of their ballistic glasses. Heads bobbed up and down like pistons as the young warriors drifted off to sleep and awakened, startled, before their eyes drooped again. Gravity was especially cruel, pulling hard on the nearly 5 pounds of each advanced combat helmet adorned with tactical lights, d-rings, para-cord, camo bands, photos of wives and babies, and night vision goggles, commonly referred to as nods.

Each of us fought a stiff neck, a sore ass, and tingling legs and feet when my gunner, Sergeant Taaga, opened the ramp. It was early February, and cold night air surrounded us as we stumbled out, rifles at the ready and adrenaline just starting to pump through our veins. We would have to worry about being tired and having aches and pains later, much later, when we are old and in our thirties. We had a mission to do.

The cold, winter night concealed our movement through a frosty grove of date palms. Our armored Stryker vehicle had deposited us along Iraq's Highway 1, at a spot some 30 miles north of Baghdad, leaving the last few klicks between us and our objective to be covered quietly on foot. The spiky trunks of date palms stood in uniform rows that disappeared into the glowing green darkness ahead. Dead and dying fronds hung low and out of place, making strange silhouettes in our night vision. Others reached up at us from their final resting places on the ground, their dry and hardened points like finely sharpened claws grabbing at our pant legs, at times puncturing fabric and flesh. Some found our faces, slicing and stinging our cold red cheeks. Decaying palm leaves, underbrush, and knee-deep ditches paralleling each row threatened at every step to give us away as we crept toward our target.

First squad was on point, walking in wide fire team wedges, with Lloyd, their squad leader, directing from the middle. The infrared strobe light in his right shoulder pocket flashed every couple of seconds, invisible to the naked eye, but clear as day in my night vision. It lit up the palms around him and left eerie snapshot profiles of the soldiers walking between us. I hoped they were on their game, as Lloyd's squad would be my over-watch when we reached our objective.

My alpha team walked between me and Lloyd's soldiers. Sergeant Fraleigh, who we often called Frolo, was at the front of his fire team wedge. Fraleigh was the best kind of guy to have as a team leader. He was a young sergeant, but he was big, loud, aggressive, and fearless. I watched him win our division's boxing championship long before he became one of my team leaders. He was the type of NCO who struck fear into the hearts of privates and Iraqis alike. No one wanted to be on his bad side.

As we walked, I spun around to check the spacing of my bravo fire team. My other team leader, Sergeant Jimmy Bridges was walking at the apex of his team's wedge. They were doing exactly what they were supposed to be doing. I was proud of my boys tonight. Their spacing was perfect, and despite all of the obstacles, we were moving silently through the palms toward our objective. It all looked like a scene from a war movie, or even a trailer for some new video game. Heavily armed soldiers moving through the darkness like silent ghosts. To the naked eye, the only evidence of their existence was the dim green glow that the night vision goggles left on their faces. All that was missing was a soundtrack by CCR and the thumping of helicopter rotor blades.

I turned back around and smiled at no one in the darkness. This was my favorite kind of mission. "Bravo Company, 1st Platoon, the "Maggots" conducts a raid against target house, vicinity Iraqi Army checkpoint, in order to kill or capture enemy sniper." My boys, second squad, would be the assaulting element, while first and third squads were to provide support and security.

I couldn't remember a time when we had walked more quietly in the dark, and I was anxious to hit this house. Just days earlier our platoon had been returning to Camp Taji after a twelve-hour patrol, when we were directed by our battalion headquarters to support our sister company, Charlie, as they searched this very home. We had hoped to make it back in time for a midnight meal at one of the Camp Taji chow halls. Instead, we set up hasty blocking positions to prevent anyone from fleeing as soldiers from Charlie Company entered and searched the house. No one had tried to run away. We sat in an empty field watching lights come on in the windows of the house and listening to the radio communication as the mission progressed. The occupants were cooperative, and there were no weapons or contraband found.

After several hours of waiting in the cold, we received instructions to hold our positions until daybreak, so that Charlie Company soldiers could search again during daylight hours. The temperatures had dropped below the freezing mark, and we sat there shivering, while frost formed around us. Finally, just before dawn, we were given permission to return to base. Charlie Company had found nothing in the home.

Now it was our turn to search this place. As we continued moving, I could make out the outline of a building through the palm trees. Lloyd, the first squad leader, whispered over the radio that he had the target house in sight. It was a pretty typical Iraqi home for this area. It was two stories with metal doors, a flat roof, and a sort of stucco exterior. There was a garage, a couple small outbuildings made of mud bricks, and a small, fenced area with goats and sheep. It was quiet and dark as we approached.

We halted and waited for Lloyd to set up his overwatch position. As he set his men in place, I whispered radio checks with Sergeant Taaga; Sergeant First Class Arambula (AB), our platoon sergeant, who had the medic; and Leo, the third squad leader. I had clear comms with everyone but Leo.

Where the hell was our reserve squad?

I walked over and knelt next to my Lieutenant. "Hey Sir, I can't get Maggot 3 on the radio. Where the hell are they? I don't even see his strobe flashing behind us."

While Lieutenant Schardt, our platoon leader, tried to raise third squad on his radio, I heard brush breaking to our right. I turned around to see what or who might be moving, and the noise grew louder.

Then Leo called out, "Hey, first platoon, where the fuck are you?"

So much for noise discipline, I thought.

"My fucking radio isn't working," he continued, almost shouting.

By this point, we had practically announced our arrival. His squad continued tromping toward us, seemingly stepping on and breaking every stick and branch in the palm grove.

I quickly walked over and whispered through clenched teeth, "Hey, shut the fuck up. What the hell is wrong with you guys?"

Leo approached and started complaining that he had been trying to get us on the radio, and that we had just left his squad alone out on the highway. He went on and on about how he had somehow ended up on the east side of the road, opposite our objective, where he ran into another platoon's blocking position while trying to figure out our location.

Finally, we got ourselves organized, and Lloyd and Leo finished getting their squads settled into overwatch and security positions. Amazingly enough, there was no sign that we had disturbed the occupants of our target house. It appeared that we still had the element of surprise working in our favor, but this whole cluster set the tone for how the assault phase of this mission would go.

I signaled for my alpha team to move forward to the house. They spread out, crouching low as they ran quietly across the clearing to the front door of the house. I followed closely behind, and as we reached the corner of the front wall the men automatically lined up in a stack. Most infantry fire teams have a breach man. In this team, it made sense for Frolo to be the door kicker. We had never encountered a door that he couldn't get through.

Sergeant Fraleigh stood in front of the door and looked at me through his night vision. I gave him a quick nod, and he took a step back with his left foot, and then slammed the heel of his boot into the door next to the latch. It gave way, but the door didn't fly open like they usually did. He kicked again. Then a third time, and the plastic mount on his night vision goggles broke. They were hanging from the para cord attached to the camo band on his helmet.

Frolo turned to me and said, "Sergeant T., my NODs are down!"

"No shit! What the fuck to do you want me to do about it? Take care of it once we get inside."

He reached up and held onto the nods while he kicked the door again. It sounded as if someone were hitting the door with a sledgehammer. It was bending in the middle, and each strike left a new dent, but it simply would not open more than a couple of inches. A light came on inside. Through a window at the top of the door, we could see a large wooden cabinet that was preventing it from opening. An outside light came on, and we no longer needed our night vision. We had also lost the benefit of surprise.

I paused for a second to figure out my next move, and a woman pulled back a window curtain and waved at us frantically. With our rifles pointed at her she motioned to the side of the house. About that time, a small boy, maybe ten or eleven years old, came walking out from around a corner and gestured for us to follow him. A man in his early forties met us at the side door and invited us in. In the main room, where Fraleigh had been kicking the door, we found a China cabinet that stood seven or eight feet high and ran the length of the room. It was full of all sorts of stuff; silver platters, little trinkets, and lots of newly broken dishes.

I called for Sergeant Bridges to bring up his team and help secure the first floor of the home. There was an elderly man, a younger man and woman, both in their late thirties, and four children ranging in age from toddler to about ten or eleven. They were cooperative but not very happy with us. The old man kept shouting at us. Our interpreter said that he wanted us to know that he was not a terrorist. He wanted to know why we were searching his home again.

We secured the first floor and separated the men from the women and children. With the help of an interpreter, I asked about any weapons in the home. The younger of the two men explained that there were two AK 47 rifles in the house and pointed to where I could find them. He said that they worked with the Sons of Iraq, and that they were allowed to have the rifles and the ammo pouches. I checked their ID cards, and they were indeed on our payroll as checkpoint security guards in that area.

That figures, I thought.

"Tell them that we are still going to search their house for weapons and contraband."

Our interpreter relayed the message and told me that they understood.

"Maggot-Six, this is Maggot-Two. Over."

"Go ahead, Maggot-Two."

"Six, first floor is secure. Moving to second floor

now. Over."

"Roger that."

Lieutenant Schardt entered the house with one of Leo's fire teams, and asked which rooms the occupants were in. I pointed to the room where the men were being held and started up the stairs with Sergeant Fraleigh and his fire team.

At the top of the stairs, there was a landing and four doors. The door to our right was metal and had a window much like the door downstairs. It was access to the roof of the home. One open door revealed a room that was mostly empty except for a few large bags of dates, presumably from the palm groves that we had just walked through. The second room was used for storage. It was piled full of all sorts of junk. I could see burlap sacks, car parts, pots and pans, broken chairs, and all kinds of other things. The door to the third room was closed.

Sergeant Fraleigh gently checked the door handle and signaled that it was locked. I nodded to him, and he kicked it. Unlike the plain metal door downstairs this door was very ornately carved wood with a brass door handle. The handle and latch mechanism fell to the floor as wood splintered around it. The door was destroyed, and the latching side of the door frame came out of the wall as well. We thought we were ready for anything as we entered and cleared rooms, but we were not prepared for what happened next.

We rushed into the room, and a man rolled out of a large bed onto the floor in front of us. A woman rolled out of the other side of the bed, taking the sheets along with her. She was screaming as she pulled the sheets up to her neck in an effort to cover herself. The man, probably in his mid-thirties, was startled and confused. He got up from the floor quickly, his eyes wide with fear and surprise. He had one hand over his head and was attempting to pull his pants up with the other. When he realized that our weapons were all pointed at him, he dropped his pants and raised his other hand. He still stood there awkwardly bent at the waist, as if he really wanted to pull his pants up, but he wasn't sure he could do it without getting shot.

A quick glance around the room confirmed what we had busted in on. His pants were around his ankles. His naked wife was curled up in a corner of the room holding a sheet up to her neck. There was a red light-bulb glowing in a wall fixture above the bed's head-board, and there was a box of peach scented douche sitting on one of the nightstands. I looked at her and then back at him, and I started laughing.

Sergeant Fraleigh laughed too and said, "That sucks dude! We had no idea you were gettin' some ass in here."

The man gave an uneasy smile. He didn't under-stand English, but he knew we were laughing at him.

I looked at the interpreter. "Tell him to pull his

fuckin' pants up. I don't want to see that shit. Tell her to get dressed too."

Once the woman was dressed, she was escorted downstairs to the room with the other woman and the children. I kept lover boy in the room so that I could ask him some questions.

"Ask him if there are any weapons in the house."

"He says that there are two AKs downstairs, and that those are the only weapons they have."

"Has he heard any gunshots in this area recently?"

"He says no."

"Ask him if he knows anything about a sniper firing on the Iraqi Army checkpoint out on the highway? I'm sure he can see the checkpoint from the roof of his house."

"He says he doesn't know anything about it."

"He's a fucking liar."

I took him downstairs and handed him off to some of the 3rd squad soldiers who were now in the house. I walked over to where Lieutenant Schardt was standing and gave him a sitrep. "The house is secure. We have two women and four children in that room. Three military-age males in this room. I'm going to start searching the place upstairs first."

"Sounds good, Sergeant T. Let me know what you find."

I walked back upstairs where Jimmy and Frolo already had their teams starting to search the rooms.

I looked around as well, watching what the soldiers were doing, and rifling through drawers and closets that hadn't been checked yet. I knew that this house had just been searched, and I wasn't very confident that we would find anything. I didn't see any reason at that point to totally trash the place.

Then I found something. In the back of the top drawer of one of the nightstands, I found a little glass dish that held about ten bullets for a 9mm handgun. Iraqis were allowed to have an AK-47 with one 30-round magazine for home protection, but there were no handguns allowed. I grabbed the dish and walked downstairs to ask lover boy about them.

Speaking to the interpreter, I asked, "Where is your handgun?"

As our interpreter spoke, he looked at me, and shook his head no.

"He says he doesn't have a handgun, only AKs."

"Why do you have ammo for a handgun if you don't have a handgun?"

"He says he doesn't have any handgun ammo either."

I showed him the dish and said, "What the fuck is this then?"

He backpedaled a bit but still insisted that there were no other weapons in the home.

"Tell him that we will leave if he just gives up the handgun."

"He still says that he doesn't have one."

I left my lieutenant to continue asking questions, while I went back to searching. We looked in all of the usual places and found nothing out of the ordinary. By this point, we were hours into the mission, and I was tired and pissed off. Captain Veath, my company commander and our first sergeant, First Sergeant Angulo were now in the house poking around and asking why we hadn't come up with anything yet. I pointed out the bullets in the dish.

Captain Veath asked, "Where is the gun?"

"I don't know," I said. "It has to be here somewhere, but they won't give it up. Without flipping this whole place upside down, I'm not sure where else to look."

"Flip this place and find it then."

"Roger that, Sir."

Back upstairs, I called all of the soldiers out of the rooms onto the landing at the top of the stairs. "We have a handful of 9mm rounds that were in a nightstand drawer in that room," I said, pointing toward the busted wooden door. "You will check every nook and cranny in this motherfucker. Flip the beds. Take the drawers out of each piece of furniture. Check the bottoms of them. Check inside to make sure that there is nothing taped above or below the drawers. Turn the furniture over and check the back and bottom of each piece. Toss everything." We broke to continue searching.

I walked into the bedroom with Private Shane Stuard. He went to the nightstand where I had found the 9mm bullets and pulled out the top drawer and dumped it. He dropped that drawer on the bed and looked into the bottom one. Then he got up and started to walk over to the closet. I told him that he needed to remove the bottom drawer, and check under and behind the nightstand too. He turned back, pulled the bottom drawer out of the nightstand, and dumped it.

"Umm, Sergeant Taylor? I think I found something."

I glanced over and saw the excited look on his face as he pulled the bag from the nightstand. He placed it on the bed and opened it. He shook his head as he reached in and pulled out a handful of 7.9mm rifle rounds.

"Nice job, Stuard! Take that out on the landing and dump it."

When he dumped the bag, hundreds of 7.9mm rifle rounds on stripper clips, and loose 7.62mm AK 47 rounds fell out onto the floor along with several loaded AK47 magazines.

I called for my lieutenant to come up, and some of my privates started organizing our find so that we could get an accurate count. When Lieutenant Schardt came up, he smiled at me, and asked if we had anything else. I told him that we still had a couple of rooms to check, and that we had found yet another

291

caliber of ammunition. I started thinking we would find more weapons.

Next was the junk room. Jimmy and I started searching this room. After finding so much ammo, we were feeling a second wind. We started pulling stuff out of the room. There were burlap sacks full of sheep's wool. It was now daylight outside, so I carried the bags out onto the rooftop. I pulled out my knife and slit the side of each bag and dumped the contents onto the cement roof.

As we moved further into the room, I found a green cylinder with white military markings on it. The cylinder was empty, but it was a shipping container for a warhead for a Brazilian surface-to-air missile. I set that aside and continued digging. Next, I found a navy-blue child's backpack with UNICEF embroidered on it. Inside the pack I found a cowboy style leather belt with bullet loops all around it. There were a few AK 47 magazines, three strands of Christmas lights with no bulbs, which are commonly used to make IEDs, and finally wrapped in a piece of cloth was a rifle scope. After moving all of these things out of the room, we reached several large rolls of canvas on the floor. They appeared to be large tents or something of that nature, but when I tried to lift one of the rolls, it was much heavier than plain canvas. I unrolled the first one, and inside I found a bolt-action rifle. I held it up for Jimmy to see. He unrolled the second roll and found a sniper rifle that went with the scope we had found. In another larger roll there was another green cylinder, this one filled with rifle cartridges for the sniper rifle. Two more rolls revealed two more rifles and two more shipping containers filled with ammo.

Jimmy and I carried the rifles and ammunition out onto the rooftop, and I called for Lieutenant Schardt, the commander, and the first sergeant. When they came through the door to the rooftop, I held up the sniper rifle and the scope.

"We didn't find a handgun, but here is your sniper rifle, Sir."

"Damn, Sergeant Taylor, we'll have to call Charlie Company and tell them that you found what they were looking for."

"No shit, Sir."

I went down to speak to the three men who had claimed that they only had two AK 47s in the house. I asked again where their handgun was. They continued to deny that anyone in the house had a handgun.

Talking to the interpreter, I said, "Okay, I believe that you don't have a handgun in the house. I have searched upstairs, and we didn't find a handgun. Are there any other weapons in the house?"

They all told the interpreter that there were no other guns in the home, and they looked relieved that I hadn't mentioned finding any weapons.

I turned to the other soldiers in the room and instructed them to put flex-cuffs on all three of the men. Once they were cuffed, I told the soldiers to bring them upstairs to the rooftop. The looks on their faces were priceless when they came through the door and saw all of the weapons and ammunition laid out across their rooftop.

In all, we discovered more than three thousand 7.62mm and 7.9mm rifle rounds, almost thirty AK-47 magazines, and seven rifles. We also had materials that were commonly used in making IEDs, and evidence that these men had gotten their hands on some sort of missiles or warheads that could have potentially been used against American soldiers in a number of different ways. It was a fruitful raid. We found what we were looking for. We accomplished our mission, to conduct a raid on the target house in order to kill or capture an enemy sniper. There was not a single shot fired, and there were no casualties, aside from some dishes and a couple of doors.

All of our success aside, I felt guilty about that raid. It was approaching lunch time by the time we had processed all of our evidence and prepared to move our three detainees. As my soldiers escorted the three handcuffed men out and placed blindfolds over their heads to protect the secret materials in our Stryker vehicles, the oldest boy came out of the front of the house. He watched armed American soldiers blindfold his father, uncle, and grandfather. His face was emotionless as the armored ramp closed, concealing the men of his family inside. My company commander walked over to him and patted him on the head. The boy's stare changed to anger and hatred when Captain Veath handed him a soccer ball.

I saw it right then: *We took his dad, and his uncle, and his grandpa, and gave him a shiny new soccer ball in return. What a fucked-up war.*

We took weapons away from insurgents, and we interfered with insurgent sniper activity in that area. What else did we do that day? Did we help reinforce negative feelings toward Americans in another generation of Iraqi people? Did we create another insurgent or another terrorist that day?

SGT SCOTT
WOLFE

THE SADR CITY
CONNECTION

by Scott Wolfe

I grew up going to Vietnam Helicopter Pilot and 101st Airborne reunions with my Dad. I was always intrigued at the connection my Dad and his friends shared. An eternal brotherhood borne out of a year or less fighting together. Those connections were not just with those with whom he flew in combat, but also with those with whom he flew out of combat. Over the years I've watched grunts and mortarmen thank my Dad and other pilots for pulling them out of some fight they would likely have died in. While they didn't know each other and might even have fought in the same area on different tours, they all shared the same common bond of fighting in the same area of operations.

Sadr City's existence as a battleground only lasted about four years, and there was not much coverage on it. At the least, you would have heard about it if you were in Iraq. Otherwise, the place was known to not many others than those who fought there. But for such an unknown area, the composition of those who fought there was quite diverse: Regular Army, Green Berets, Navy SEALs, Marine Advisors with Kurdish ICDC, and the Air Force... Ground troops and Aviation alike. Every nationality you can think of. All American.

I was fortunate enough to deploy with people I had already known for a few years. It was not until fighting in Sadr City that I began to understand what putting differences aside really meant. It didn't matter who called on the radio (whether or not you'd have a beer with them back home): we went without a second thought if they called for tank support. If a tank went down, that tank was surrounded by other tanks until we could tow them out. It was all about the willingness to take a life in order to save another American. It was all about functioning in situations where the entire world has shrunk to just you and those with whom you are fighting. It was just you and your Brothers living a lifetime together inside a year.

Those of us in Aces Tank Company went different ways after OIF II. We kept in touch where possible, but most weren't able to really reconnect until social media came about. As the connections happened, the excitement of seeing everyone grew in working together to track each other down. While traveling for my job, I was able to meet up with Aces Brothers on occasion. It wasn't until September of 2019, though, that several of us got to meet up for a first reunion in Texas. It was there that I experienced what I saw among my father and his battle buddies while growing up. Not seeing some of these guys for fifteen years, we had the ability to talk like we had seen each other just a week prior. The connection never faded.

In October 2020 at the filming of Tara Thompson's music video Sadr City, I met guys from other units that fought in Sadr City after I did. I was amazed at how quickly everyone started e talking and connecting. I had always known that other units were in Sadr City, but it wasn't until that day I learned how bad they had it as well. This is where I experienced that extended connection I saw at 101st reunions with Dad. I gained 100s of Brothers that day. Brothers I have yet to meet but share that Sadr City connection with that only we can understand.

Months later, it is still a profound and emotional experience to me. I want to meet as many as I can and shake the hand of everyone who fought there and made it home. I want to help connect everyone from every branch from every MOS that spent time there. I want to tell my piece of the Sadr City saga.

I want every #sadrcityboy to know they are my Brother.

Sadr City
THE MUSIC VIDEO

In August 2020 singer-songwriter Marc Christian called neighbor Robbie Grayson about a new song he co-authored with recording artist Tara Thompson: *Sadr City*. Robbie had Marc on the phone in minutes with Boone Cutler, Warfighter and author of *CallSign Voodoo*, his 2005|2006 autobiography of his service in Sadr City. Within days Christian and Tara Thompson decided to shoot a music video. Robbie's house would be the location, and Cutler would send the call out over social media to #SadrCityBoys in the vicinity to come be a part of the video. On October 16, 2020 all of the coordination paid off and the *Sadr City* music video was shot.

This section of *Angels in Sadr City: We Remember* is a tribute to Tara Thompson, Marc Christian, the musicians and producer who made the music and video happen in time for Veterans Day 2021.

Thank you!

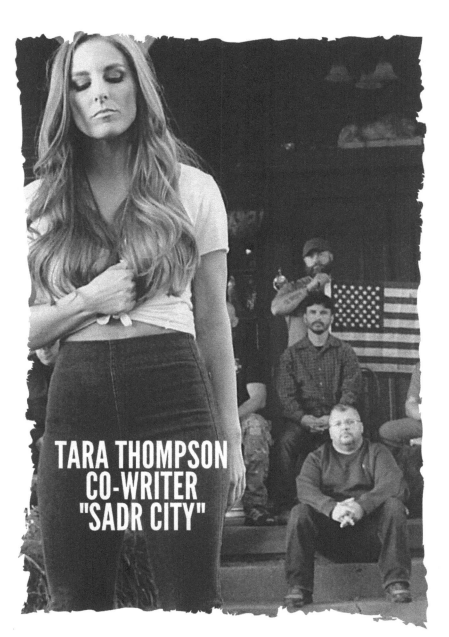

TARA THOMPSON
CO-WRITER
"SADR CITY"

**MARC CHRISTIAN
CO-WRITER
"SADR CITY"**

DAVE RISTRIM
STEEL GUITAR

JAMES COOK
BASS GUITAR

DAN
COHEN
ELECTRIC &
ACOUSTIC GUITARS

KENT
SLUCHER
DRUMS &
PERCUSSION

TARA
THOMPSON
WRITER & VOCALIST

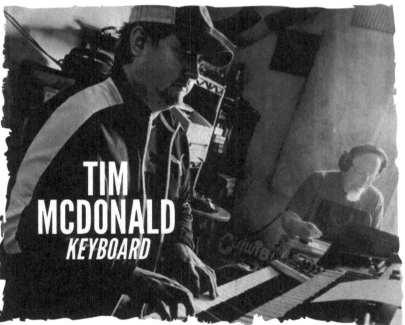

TIM
MCDONALD
KEYBOARD

Sadr City Music & Video Team

★ ★ ★ ★ ★

Tara Thompson, Marc Christian
Writers

Dan Cohen
Electric & Acoustic Guitar

James Cook
Bass Guitar

Kent Slucher
Drums & Percussion

Dave Ristrim
Steel Guitar

Tim McDonald
Keyboard

Marc Christian, James Cook
Background Vocals

James Cook
Production/Engineering

Download *Sadr City*
from the following platforms

www.tarathompson.com

Lightning Source UK Ltd.
Milton Keynes UK
UKHW041242301221
396388UK00001B/23

9 781088 011140